MANY
BRAVE
FOOLS

MANY

A Story of Addiction, Dysfunction, Codependency...

BRAVE

...and Horses

FOOLS

SUSAN E. CONLEY

TRAFALGAR SQUARE
North Pomfret, Vermont

First published in 2019 by
Trafalgar Square Books
North Pomfret, Vermont 05053

Some names and identifying details have been changed to protect the privacy of individuals.

Disclaimer of Liability
The author and publisher shall have neither liability nor responsibility to any person or entity with respect to any loss or damage caused or alleged to be caused directly or indirectly by the information contained in this book. While the book is as accurate as the author can make it, there may be errors, omissions, and inaccuracies.

Trafalgar Square Books encourages the use of approved safety helmets in all equestrian sports and activities.

Library of Congress Cataloging-in-Publication Data
Library of Congress Cataloging-in-Publication Data
Names: Conley, Susan, author.
Title: Many brave fools : a story of addiction, dysfunction, codependency, and horses / Susan E Conley.
Description: North Pomfret, Vermont : Trafalgar Square Books, 2018.
Identifiers: LCCN 2018019737| ISBN 9781570768873 (pbk.) | ISBN 9781570769269
  (ebook)
Subjects: LCSH: Conley, Susan. | Horsemanship--Therapeutic use. |
  Codependents--Biography. | Drug addicts' spouses--Biography. | Horsemen
  and horsewomen--Biography. | LCGFT: Autobiographies.
Classification: LCC RM931.H6 C66 2018 | DDC 616.89/16581--dc23
LC record available at https://lccn.loc.gov/2018019737

Front cover photograph by Diana DeMari; author photo by Mike Blackett/
Smashbox Cosmetics
Book design by Tim Holtz
Cover design by RM Didier
Typefaces: Marion, Arial
Printed in the United States of America
10 9 8 7 6 5 4 3 2 1

A BIG PAT

Mercury, Argo, Delilah, Rebel, Tango, Murdo, Rinaldo, Ruby,
Spike, Billy, Jack, Apollo, Bingo, Guy, Colt, Bari, Guapo,
Hernando, Gracie, Jack, Morris, Jim, Connell, William, Paddy,
Noodles, Soprano, Simba, Commanche, Verdi, Snipe, Harry, Nero,
Milton, Ebony, Bonnie, Archie, Freya, Elsa, Luigi, Kiwi, and Rom

CONTENTS

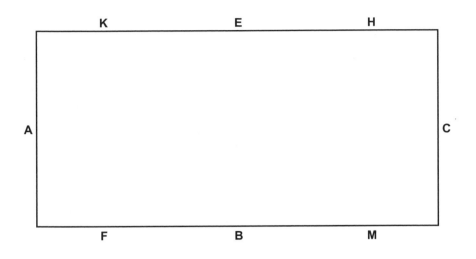

All King Edward's Horses Carry Many Brave Fools

Mnemonic for the letters used at strategic areas in the riding arena (pictured) for dressage tests, as told to me by one of my instructors

MOUNT

What's the point of riding in circles, over and over, on horse-back? It's a question that springs to mind when riding the umpteenth "twenty-meter circle" in a lesson. This shape is a foundational figure in dressage, a riding discipline concerned with demonstrating the suppleness and responsiveness of the horse, and it's integral to the education of both horse and rider. There are myriad ways to ride it: in walk, in trot, in canter; at one end of the arena and then the opposite; or the most challeng-ing, in the middle where the horse can't hug the perimeter fence on half of it.

At the start of a horseback riding career, such circles aren't ridden so much as endured; the school horse is most likely following the one in front of him or her by rote, requiring little from the rider, and indeed, the rider has little to give—at that stage. She is happy enough to *not* fall off, and the whole riding-in-a-circle thing feels safe. She goes with the flow, hopes the instructor has something nice to say, and if not, that's okay, too. It's not as though she has a clue as to how to change anything she is doing, because she really isn't doing much of anything at all.

Most non-horsey people's impressions of horseback rid-ing may come from movies and television shows, during which

cowboys or medieval-types are tearing about the place brandish-
ing weaponry; trotting (a relatively slow pace) in a circle over and
over seems laughable at best, pathetic at worst.

It's just not very dramatic.

What's the point of doing *anything* over and over? That
depends. Does learning result? Or does repetition encourage
zoning out, a mental disengagement that allows one—say, a
woman in a dysfunctional marriage—to pretend certain things
aren't happening? The woman perhaps sees what is unfolding in
her primary relationship and refuses on some level to accept it,
and so begins to live a life of dissociation, of fantasy, of absence,
because frankly, reality is crap. Hoping is much better; hope
means that things might transform in some miraculous way,
because actual hands-on change seems as unlikely as winning the
lottery. Actual change is frightening because it requires action
and decision-making and uncertainty. Also, there is a rhythm to
the days and weeks of that life that is entirely predictable, as the
same things happen over and over and over. The woman knows
exactly what to do almost all the time. It is familiar, and despite
being painful, it is safe.

What's the point of a memoir? What's the value of going
over and over the same old story? That depends, too. I began
horseback riding in order to recover from a marriage in which
my partner's substance misuse triggered my codependency issues.
By finding my way to a barn and onto the back of a horse, I was
allowing myself to do something that I thought I'd like to try, but
never had. I had been so busy, for so long, trying to get somebody
else to do things differently, I had no time for myself, alone. If
I was off on my own, I had no idea what *he* was up to. If I took
time for myself, I wouldn't be with him, monitoring his mood,
doing what I thought was needed to improve it if it was despon-
dent, or to enjoy it if it was ebullient. I was always prepared for

something to go wrong, because something invariably did, like the raging fallout from another lost job, or the time he engaged in an aggressive staring contest with a gang of rough inner-city lads while portentously stroking the blade of small box cutter, on a bus, which he got off first, leaving me behind to sit with the pack of threatened, angry young men. I guess he reckoned I'd take care of it, because that's what I did.

When I did finally decide to leave the relationship, I was equally alarmed and buoyed by my daring. I needed a distraction, and the idea of hopping up on the back of an enormous animal I had no experience controlling seemed to fit the bill. I'd been foolishly trying to control someone else's addiction for years, so how hard could it be?

It *was* hard, and scary...but so unlike anything I'd ever done before that it was also fascinating, engrossing, and eventually, less petrifying.

An inveterate keeper-of-journals, I surprised myself when I didn't immediately begin documenting my new adventure; in the past, I routinely sought to transcribe the meaning of my experiences. Journaling had also been a terrific way to separate myself from people, places, and things (the better to complain about them), which paradoxically allowed me to distance myself from my own narrative without doing much to change my circumstances. My equine undertaking was entirely different: I was so focused on riding horses that I didn't have time to be omniscient, nor did I have the desire to be anything but present. I was utterly enthralled with my new lifestyle—and it *was* a lifestyle, effecting changes in what I wore, what I ate, and whether or not I accepted a social invitation the night before a riding lesson. And I was so captivated by the things that I was learning I didn't need to write about it. I was content to do it, plain and simple, without turning it into a story.

When I did start to blog about my experiences, one year on from my very first lesson, it was in an effort to share, rather than hide, what was happening to me. I barely understood it myself: I traveled hours to get to the equestrian center via two buses. I engaged in an activity that was sometimes pretty danger-ous. I bought things with names like "half chaps" and "schooling whips." And I read everything I could about horses, to find out why they were the way they were and how they got that way. As I distilled the highs and lows of it all, I saw that there was more to this thing than keeping my heels down and my shoulders back. Something else was happening, on many levels, and I began to investigate what that meant to me. I realized that my desire to dredge up my marital peaks and valleys was limited to the ways in which I had reacted to them, rather than trying to deconstruct what had been going on with my partner.

The memories as presented in this book aren't linear, one event after the next. Maybe this imperfect recollection is the product of denial or dissociation. Maybe it's a healthy desire to keep the focus on myself as I figure out how it transpired that someone else's well-being became the sole condition through which I permitted myself to have a sense of security in the world. I do recall the atmosphere, the codependent fog through which I moved, and that figures largely in the following pages.

I eventually got a little bit better at riding twenty-meter circles and started to understand how I could effect change in the riding of them. I recognized that riding all the way up the back end of another horse in a group lesson wasn't terribly safe, so I began to nudge my mount into a slightly larger circle to move him away and gain some space between us and the horse ahead. I realized that riding a circle in trot and riding one in canter was, um, kind of different, and that the latter required that I do even more things on top of the myriad actions I was already taking. I discovered that sometimes, simply walking a horse in a circle was the most difficult thing of all.

I also came to understand that not all quarters of the circle were the same, that maybe the horse was grand on the first but started collapsing inward on the second or third, and was completely cutting around the fourth in order to get back to the track next to the arena fence. I started to anticipate this and correct for it before it happened. And when I did, and stopped the collapsing from happening, even if a non-horsey observer wouldn't notice any great difference, *I* knew the difference, and that was all that mattered.

Twelve years on, when I work on my circles in a riding lesson, it may look like I'm doing the same thing over and over, and I am, but I actually am not. I mean, it's still a circle, but it's the riding of it that matters. Sometimes the horse is supple and in great form, sometimes he is stiff and grumpy; the same goes for me. Sometimes we float around the arena, wonderfully in tune; sometimes the first circle of the lesson goes horribly wrong, and the rest of the hour becomes a power struggle between human and animal. It's during the latter situation that the most growth occurs: when one quarter, then a half, then three quarters of the circle slowly start to come good, I've learned what is needed to keep the horse fluid and balanced, and learned how to keep getting it, over and over. The subtlety in the improvement of my circles becomes an independent pursuit; while it can be judged and praised by the instructor, the task ultimately becomes my own responsibility, and my own joy.

Like this book, my healing process has not followed a linear trajectory. I didn't wake up one day, decide I'd like my life to improve, go back to the beginning, and start all over. Instead, something would happen that triggered a thought, a feeling, a memory, and I'd look at it and decide how to deal with it, and whether or not I was *able* to deal with it. I would slip back, sometimes, into a dissociative state (one of my favorite coping mechanisms), and wait for myself to be ready to face it and try again. And so the story of both my riding and my recovery goes back and forth in time, evoking a scene here, a feeling there, a reaction all over the place, falling in on the third quarter, running out on the fourth, until slowly, the whole thing becomes conscious and balanced. Success occurs when each of the four quarters flows smoothly into one another, when you can't see the join between each quadrant. The structure of this narrative is very much the same as riding those circles, revisiting and reconciling, until the movement around the remembrance is solely focused on my actions, my participation, the part I played in it all. Then, it corrects itself, through clarity and experience, until it flows smoothly, gently, into the present.

I am a regular person. I was not born in the saddle. I didn't even get near a saddle until I reached "middle age." It never occurred to me, as a child, to pine for a horse. I don't manage a barn, I don't compete at a high level, I don't even own my own horse (yet). What I *do* do is give this pursuit my all; here, I provide a window into what it's like to try something new well into midlife, and a glimpse of the benefits of having a passion, no matter one's age. To paraphrase a well-known quote, the outside of a horse has become very good for the inside of this woman, in ways I'd never dreamed possible.

CHAPTER ONE

SHIT

When you're in the shit—seriously in the emotional shit—face down, immobilized, prostrate in it, it is actually comforting. After all, everything that's led up to the chaos, fear, pain, and uncertainty required adrenaline and attention. Once the threshold from indecision to decision is crossed—for isn't all the chaos, fear, pain, and uncertainty created in indecision?—the relief of being down in the muck is simply incalculable.

For that's when you are absolved of all emotional duties: you don't have to fix anything anymore, or worry. You may worry that you are not worrying, but soon, even that is too exhausting. You are down for the count, and it is bliss.

In the shit, you will find your rest.

And once rested, if you're really, really lucky, you get up and do something wonderful.

Shit is everywhere in an equestrian facility. Certainly, during the hour before a horse's stall is mucked out, you can find yourself up to your ankles in manure. You go in to fetch your designated ride for a lesson, and there it is, all over the stable, tiny dolmens of poo piled up with disregard to placement or convenience.

For the human, anyway. For the horse, what could be more convenient than pooping where he stands?

One learns quickly to disregard the manure; it is the most natural thing in the world. After all, horses in the field eat for an average of sixteen to twenty hours a day. Despite her best efforts, when I was taking a few stable-management lessons from one of my instructors, she began to despair of teaching me anything else after I had learned this fact. Twenty hours? No wonder they are capable of releasing almost fifty pounds of excrement a day. Now, only twelve-and-a-half pounds of it is solid, but still. That's a lot of smelly stuff.

It's a smell, though, that doesn't stink. Not when you go horse-crazy.

Let's say I've had a bad day. The kind that started from the moment I set foot on the pavement in the morning and followed me through the work day, into the traffic that evening, which appeared to have backed up just for me personally, so that I'd be late for my riding lesson. Let's say that the cocktail of emotions swirling around my psyche involved dissatisfaction, frustration, sadness, resentment, and pain. Every single unpleasant thing— every pointless argument, every gutting loss—disintegrates with the first whiff: sharp and pungent, the fragrance has top notes of pee and poo and hay, a soupçon of horse breath, and the subtle nuances of horsey skin, horsey mane, cat, dog, earth, and bedding. Nothing and nowhere else smells exactly like it, not the zoo, nor the New York subway in August at midday, even though one might roughly assign the same alchemical qualities to both environs.

Often, the only thing that stands between me and the poison of an extraordinarily foul day is the remembrance of that first whiff of equine micturition on a cold winter's night in the Dublin Mountains. It smells of heat, and life, and it is as comforting as a hug, as soothing as a hand running down your hair, as joyful as a phone call to your best friend in the world.

I took up horseback riding at the tender age of forty-two, and knowing I had a lot to catch up on, I figured I'd better learn how to shovel shit.

I asked one of my friends from the barn (in Ireland, where I began this adventure, we called it "the yard") if she knew how to "muck out" a stall, as they say around horses.

She said she did, so I asked her how you did it.

She looked a little dubious and said, "I could tell you, but you really have to do it for yourself, Sue."

Yeah. I thought as much. And sobering words indeed from a fifteen-year-old. There really aren't any shortcuts in the horse world.

I'd already looked up mucking on the Internet. You needed a pitchfork, if you were going to be mucking out straw bedding, or a shavings fork if you used sawdust or wood shavings instead. (I had to Google "shavings fork" because I couldn't imagine how the two might differ. It looked like a comb, having about three times as many tines as a pitchfork.)

Okay, so, you took the horse out, then you went back into the stall and started using the correct fork—no, wait, you needed a wheelbarrow as well, and it was suggested that you point it in the direction of the manure pile before you began, because, well, it probably saved time, I supposed. With the fork you picked up whatever bedding was soiled and dumped it into the wheelbarrow. Then you spread the remaining unsoiled stuff evenly around the stall, and added clean bedding. Next you swept a little bit, even though they didn't put a broom on the checklist, and you put your horse back in his stall prior to wheeling the muck away.

My attention started to drift by the time the instructions were telling me to spread the bedding, because how did you know how much to put down? And besides, what was the story of what went underneath the bedding? Plain concrete seemed stingy, and I'd seen padding and sand and who knows what. Plus when I'd Googled the shavings fork, I got distracted...there were so many options! There was the T-grip, the D-grip, and the textured grip. You could choose from a long handle or a short handle or a fiberglass handle. It seemed apparent you couldn't just grab a fork and start mucking—or you could, but perhaps it would be uncomfortable, a strain on your back, say, if you used a short-handled D-grip and it didn't suit you.

I had watched the grooms at the stable as they went about this mysterious business. It seemed like they just grabbed a thing—a fork thing—and started forking. Or a shovel, which was also suggested in my Internet instructions under certain circumstances, and my God, you should see the world of shovels out there.

When you don't know what you are doing, it can be overwhelming.

When you don't know what you are doing, and you want to know about it more than anything else you can remember wanting to know, then it is dazzling.

This is a book about my shit, mine and mine alone.

For a codependent person like me, this is a massive statement. When you're a codependent personality, the story is never about you. The story is always about the other person: his problems, her feelings, their well-being. That other person is also quite often, though not always, an addict of some description. The codependent is the enabler who, well, enables the addict to avoid suffering the slings and arrows of the outrageous misfortunes that he creates, often to the detriment of his safety and well-being, on every level. Emotionally, mentally, spiritually, and physically, the codependent sacrifices her health, calls it love, and quite often, though not always, becomes a land mine of rage and frustration waiting to explode.

As for me, I was waiting for my award. A codependent like me is, of course, only doing everything out of love, but you know, a little recognition would be nice, once in a while: How about some gratitude for paying all the bills—again? How about a little appreciation for finding you a job—again? Would it kill you to say thanks, and mean it, from the heart?

It might. Because at times it seems that it would absolutely kill the codependent to let the other person live his life, with all its consequences.

Much of my experience of living as a codependent had to do with the idea that I was only as important as someone else's problems. The other person—it didn't have to be my husband, it could be a friend, or a coworker—had a problem, and I immediately began to have ideas about how to solve it. I was the one who always managed, the one who had all the answers. It was so satisfying to have answers, and not just some answers: *all* of them. It was like being Einstein, Mother Teresa, and the Oracle at Delphi, all rolled into one, because you got to be a genius, a saint, and a sage simultaneously. It was brilliant to see so clearly and to always be right.

You can never be more "right" than when you hook up with someone with substance misuse issues. Someone who drinks too much is drunk a lot of the time and someone who does drugs is out looking for them, or asleep, or somewhere else being *awake awake awake*, and tends not to tend to any responsibilities and commitments. In both cases, they clearly need someone to do shit for them.

Doing shit for someone in that condition opens up a whole new world of being right about just about everything, all the time, 24/7/365. You can't count on him being there to do much, most of the time, because he is mostly off his head, or thinking about being off his head, or coping with the fallout of recently having been off his head. He is barely functioning, while you are functioning like the Hoover Dam: indestructible, holding back the tide. He can't hold down a job, so he never has any money—except to buy the substance of choice. You wonder where that money comes from, so you begin to hide your wallet, to walk around with your money tucked in your bra, just in case. The bra area is safe as houses, because sex is an early casualty of the interaction between codependent and addict. It becomes something to withhold, a bargaining chip, a power play, yet another situation that you know will change for the better when the other person changes for the better.

Things go from bad to worse, but this is not insurmountable for Super Capable Wonder Woman. You know exactly what your beloved addict needs to do: he needs to stop being addicted! Since he is too distracted by his own shit, then obviously you are the one capable of getting him clean and sober. Since you are so good at everything, it shouldn't take long. You sit him down, and you tell him how much you care for him and that life has become untenable for you because he is no longer present in the relationship, and you feel that something has to change. He needs to get help, and you want to help him in every way you can so that your life together can be good again.

This is not a bad speech. In fact, it's a very brave speech, a terrifically hard one to make, because people-pleasing codependents are generally not so good with the truth. You surmount your honesty obstacle, he promises to seek recovery, and damn, you have really knocked this shit out of the park!

12

The Speech is so good that you just can't help but deliver it a second time, and a third time, and a fourth time. The Speech keeps getting better and better each time you give it; it gets blacker and whiter, tougher, less compromising, and it grows in length and banked fury until one day, all you do is speech-ify. Every single thing out of your mouth turns into an oration of some sort or other. "Pass the ketchup" becomes fraught with meaning and portent. You discourse and pontificate because if your loved one would only listen then you wouldn't have to keep saying the same thing over and over...but you say the same thing over and over because, you are certain, it's got to sink in at some stage. And once it sinks in, your partner will change, and then your life won't be total crap.

I took to lurking around the barn at mucking time, pretending to talk to a horse that was in a stall next to one that was get-ting a going over. One day, I spied on a kid who was "skipping out." I had read about skipping out: using the fork-y thing from the Internet, all he was doing was sifting out the poo from the bedding, and chucking it in a "muck bucket." This process only scratches the surface; it is maintenance. Since most stabled horses don't eat as much as those out wandering green meadows, they don't produce all that manure (twelve-and-a-half pounds a day!), and it's unnecessary to start from square one every time.

It doesn't pay, though, to let it build up.

Square one, my-marriage-wise, was returned to several times a year. I could set my watch by it. There would be a time of joy and fun and wonderful union, followed by a time of gradual decline instigated by a binge on pharmaceuticals, which created a big, black, horrible vacuum that sucked all the life and light out of the relationship. There were cues; I picked them up like I was on Broadway. The Cycle lasted for a fortnight and followed the same bullet points without fail:

1) It began with a gradual withdrawal from easy, quotidian conversation between us (two days).
2) There would be a descent into heavy silence that felt suffocating. During this time (four days), a room was never big enough to contain both of us, so he would get up and leave if I entered.
2a) Along with the above, a general disregard for my belongings presented itself, to the degree that I was tempted to hide my laptop.
3) Next came a spate of excessive sleep (three more days).
4) Despite the fog of the drugs, there was grudging effort to return (one day).
5) Instead of rushing in to help pull him over the edge of the cliff, I attempted to stay detached (about five minutes).
6) Then there was a day or two of promises and tears (this was where The Speech came in), and then two days of actual physical and mental return to the land of the living.

As the years went on, I began to see that The Speech wasn't a monologue, but a dialogue: I felt almost guided into giving it, that I was being manipulated, via the silence, by the force of his disregard, because it was such an integral part of the insanity. If I didn't give The Speech, we wouldn't start all over again. The Speech was the point in The Cycle in which I could sense the effects of my partner's binge were starting to taper off, and I was afraid to deviate from the program. I was afraid that if I left out one tiny bit, even so much as one word, we'd never come all the way back, that I was a shit wife for letting it all fall apart—that it would be all my fault.

It was seven on a frosty morning. I could see my breath, see the moon, bright as a knife, see its light glimmer off the dew that had turned to ice, making the pavement glitter and the grass crackle. It was January, but January in Ireland, and this was extreme cold for these parts. In the twenty years I'd lived there, the winter of 2011 was the first in which snow and ice figured so prominently. Usually, I passed the season wearing little more than a bulky sweater and knit poncho, but this year the frigidity was too reminiscent of my East Coast, USA, upbringing. I had not moved here for this.

If nothing else, the cold woke me up. It wasn't that I hated mornings; I got my best sleep between seven and nine. But I'd rise early for the horses, and that morning I was on my way to Bray, Co Wicklow, to learn how to muck out.

The night before, I'd thought about canceling. I hadn't received confirmation that there was someone who'd teach me, and I didn't want to get all the way out there and find my journey had been in vain. I also felt like I was maybe getting a little bit sick? Maybe? It was rather like the very first riding lesson that I ever took—I had wanted to put that off, as well, to defer beginning. There was always something about learning a new skill that created a wee tingle of fear, enough that you wanted to delay it, avoid it, never do it at all.

Then I got the confirmation email and went to bed early.

There was a bright star on the horizon, or maybe it was Venus or Jupiter. I leaned against the frosty fence that separated the pavement and Dublin Bay, and hoped to God that the bus would be on time, because my ass was starting to freeze. I had considered wearing jeans rather than my jodhpurs; I wasn't sure what other people wore when they mucked. I didn't bring gloves, which was starting to feel like a stupid thing to forget, and then it occurred to me that I might not have enough layers on. Whenever I'd ridden in similar weather, a long-sleeved T-shirt was plenty sufficient, but I wasn't going to be getting any heat from the horse, or from the movements associated with riding. I had slung on a thermal undershirt, but was that going to suffice? I didn't want to shovel in my bulky coat—I'd have no range of movement at all...

Two buses and a three-quarter mile hike down an icy road later, I arrived, having decided to leave off the coat but wear my scarf and knit cap. I wasn't sure what to do when my contact person wasn't at her desk. I went into the locker room to put on my boots, which were warm and specifically designed for mucking about the barn. This was exciting, as I'd never worn them for their express purpose until then. I'd had them for two years.

A woman came up to me and introduced herself as Sally. "I'll be showing you how to muck," she said, and I followed her to the shed to collect a pitchfork, a shavings fork, and a muck bucket, all my own. The bucket looked like a laundry basket, with an open lattice-weave embossed on plastic; it was flexible with two small handles on the top. I was delighted to be carrying a shavings fork and bucket. There were many grooms around, carrying forks and buckets, and now, I could count myself as one of them. I set the bucket down outside one of the ponies' stalls, and tightened my scarf. I was ready.

Sally said, "First, we fork the bedding like this." She proceeded to expertly flip the shavings so they shored up against the walls, and in the process she lobbed hidden little balls of poo all over the place. "The droppings just start to fling up," she observed as she moved efficiently around the enclosure.

I knew how to deal with those little balls of poo! My hands tightened around the handle of my shavings fork in anticipation. But then, Sally dug deep into the bedding with the pitchfork.

"Now you have to dig down, flip it over, and throw the big bits in there." She dug, flipped, and there was a solid piece of whatever *it* was—mud, bedding, feed, shit? All of the above? —fused together by pee. It was damp, and yes, "mucky," and she slung the most solid parts into the bucket.

"Then you use *that* on the droppings," she said, nodding to my shavings fork. "Make sure to get them all."

All of them? I thought, because there were a lot of them. The bits of poo came in a variety of sizes, and they were everywhere. I lifted the fork (it was seriously heavy in and of itself) and dug in for my first scoop.

Well, I had a lot of stuff on the fork, including bedding that really needn't go, so I shook the fork, and the shake was too hard, and everything fell off the tines. I scooped again, and jiggled it just a little. This time, the poo bounced all over the place...*then* fell off. Sally was over in the corner doing something else, and I felt pressured. I wasn't doing it right and was beginning to think the whole thing was really a bad idea.

I scooped and shimmied the fork, wiggling my elbow and keeping my wrist locked. The shavings fell off and the droppings remained. Victorious, I deposited them in the bucket and scooped again.

Sally was flicking another round of shavings up against the wall, and I saw more of the poo balls flying through the air. I kept scooping, and skimming, and the bucket filled, until soon we'd loaded two buckets full of muck. Then, Sally redistributed the bedding that had been turned up. She pulled some of the stuff down from the walls; suddenly, the ground was level again, and we were done.

Sally said to set the full buckets by the door, as someone would come by with a wheelbarrow and empty them. I dragged one out of the stall and left it on a slight concrete incline leading into the stable aisle, and was about to walk away, move on to the next one, when I realized leaving the bucket in this position, off balance, might be precarious. It wouldn't do to have it spill everything all over the place, would it? I didn't want to have to shovel the same shit twice.

I started the next stall on my own. I dealt with the big piles of poo, shoveling it out and dropping it into the bucket. I took off my knit cap and stuffed it into a pocket. My hair was as drenched as if I had been riding in a lesson. I wielded the shavings fork, piling dry stuff up against the walls. I got into a rhythm and the pile grew, as I soon began to scoop the droppings. This became a soothing, almost hypnotic procedure. I found that if I shook the fork, and also gave it a little bounce that initiated from my shoulder, the separation of droppings-from-bedding went faster. I began to like my bouncy-shake, and felt that I'd found my signature move.

I paused and loosened my scarf. The sun was fully out, as bright as the moon had been, with not a cloud in the sky. Wheelbarrows rolled by, people stopped to say hello and ask me if I was working there for the day. I explained that I'd never mucked out before and wanted to learn. "Good for you," they all said, and walked on as I went back to scooping and flinging. I was sweating, but I was on a roll, and my breathing had settled down.

Then Sally came back, took up the pitchfork, and started digging down.

Ah. I'd forgotten that part.

I apologized, and she said it was no big deal, but the mare whose stall it was, happened to be as enthusiastic a pee-er as she was a poo-er, and man, that stuff was heavy. I dug, and dug, and

18

dug. My breath became short again, and as I bent, my shoulders started to burn. I breathed, and tried not to berate myself for forgetting the part where you really had to go underneath. As with many things, the stuff that was on the surface was the least of it.

I would know without fail when we were about to enter The Cycle again, even before I was fully conscious. I'd wake every morning, already scanning my environment, gauging the atmosphere. Would I be greeted with a hot cup of coffee on the bedside table, a companionable sit-down next to me on the mattress, an endearment, a kiss? Or would I wake and tense at the sound of dishes being resentfully washed in the sink, which was directly below my head, one floor down? There'd be no coffee in this case, no kiss. The desire to go back to sleep was robust in these moments, and often I succumbed to it. The need for caffeine was overwhelmed by the powerful desire to stay hidden upstairs until the coast was clear.

Or would I wake to the sound of labored breathing beside me, a sleep so deep that nothing would rouse him from it, not even the alarm? Would I steadily raise the volume, keep hitting the snooze, keep sounding the alert that it was almost time, verging on getting late to get up for work? Would I make the coffee, bring it upstairs, watch the cup on the nightstand turn cold, as my companionable sit-down on the mattress finally inspired movement: a turned back, a rejection of connection?

I would see it for what it was, but I couldn't leave it alone. When he finally left for the job he was starting to hate, and I had the house to myself, I would start digging around, looking for whatever it was that he was using...this time. I doubted anyone I knew would ever picture me in such a scenario, on my knees, pawing through the back of a closet, one ear out for the key in the door. On the surface, marriage-wise, things looked normal, as far as the picture we presented to the world was concerned. In private, though, my need to control, which was often held at manageable levels and channeled through my own work, became utterly *un*manageable. I did stuff, stuff like checking the pockets of all his coats, that it was not my business to do. I thought I was doing it out of love, but it was out of a need to know, to find out the things I was sure he wasn't telling me.

I was constantly dwelling on what had happened and when; then, as things got really bad, I started worrying about what *might* happen, so that I could figure out ahead of time how to deal with it. I would lurch from crisis to crisis, and sometimes it seemed we'd both reached the end of our tethers at the same time. Then we'd cry and hold each other, and promise to do better, to be better, to stop all the bingeing and the whingeing. Things would be okay for a little while—and then the tether would go slack, and mysteriously extend itself, silently, in the night maybe, while we were sleeping, and The Cycle would start, inevitably, all over again.

It was possible to do this for a lifetime. I could have done it forever. I was in my early forties, had married late—how would I ever meet anyone else if I left him?

What if I left, and he got well without me?

What then?

When I found myself capable of this thought—that he might be better *without me*—was when I realized the part I played in the madness. Up to that point, I was more than happy to blame everything on his patently bad behavior. Up to that point, I would never admit my choices might have been equally as awful. Up to that point, I was too afraid to detach, fully and completely, from the situation. Then I had that thought, and I let nature take its course. I allowed the thing, the inexorable, soul-destroying, painful thing we had created together, to spin out of control entirely.

From somewhere deep down, I dug in, and stopped.

I dug and turned the bedding, dumping the big, gummy bits in the bucket, which I emptied into the wheelbarrow someone had left outside the stall. I returned to dig and dig some more. Sally came in and started to spread and level the remaining bedding, and as she forked the stuff up against the wall again, she said, "Look, they're just flinging out."

Shit! There were more droppings! I muttered an apology, and took up the shavings fork again, my bouncy-shake move less assured before a witness. I fumbled, I dropped poo, I forked up too much dry bedding.

"Look, they're just flinging out," she repeated, and I felt a flare of anger. Okay, got it! Not perfect! I had my doubts that you could actually get them all—maybe you just needed to do the best you could and cut your losses.

"I thought I got them all," I mumbled. Sally just laughed and said it happened all the time.

She brought in a bale of fresh shavings and left me to break them up and spread them out. I lashed into the bale with the fork, and the clean brightness of them spread like a carpet of absolute purity. I shifted them around, and my actions felt supportive, comfortable—clean. There may have been some droppings lurking, but all in all, I thought I'd done a good job.

The thing about mucking is, it's an end in and of itself. You can't make a perfect stall, because once the horse gets back in, he's going to do what he wants to do anyway. The horse may even pee all over the place again, immediately, to make the space his own. There will be more droppings. You will have to do it all over again tomorrow. Yet it isn't an exercise in futility: it's all about clearing the deck for the next round, because there is *always* a next round. It's all about how you choose to frame it. If you're going for perfection, then you're going to be disappointed.

I was meant to muck my last stall with Luna, a mare, still in it, because sometimes you have to work around the horse. However, a teen came in to groom Luna at the same time, and the mare found the combination of flying pitchfork and mane-pulling a bit much. It was kind of like if you were hanging out in your bathroom and someone came in to clean it, and then someone else came in and started to do your hair.

Nina expressed her stress and annoyance by lifting her tail ("Nina!" her hair stylist moaned) and taking a massive dump.

I had to laugh. When the mare lifted her near hind leg ("Nina, don't step in it!" the girl scolded) and stepped in it...well, there was nothing I could do, was there? I had to simply wait until the poo cooled down and then fork it into the bucket.

Hand on my heart: it truly didn't bother me. But let me tell you, in the past? Shit like that would have made me crazy.

CHAPTER TWO

CRAZY

I've heard it said that insanity can be defined as "doing the same thing over and over, yet expecting a different result." If you look at it like that, then the horseback riding and the codependency business both have an element of crazy, but to different degrees. In both cases, someone on the outside might look at what's going on and think, "That is some crazy shit." The thing with horses is, while it looks like the same thing is happening over and over again, it actually is not.

For example: I had one lesson in which all we did was circles, in trot, for thirty minutes. We rode twenty-meter circles at one end of the arena, at the other end, in the center, on the left rein, on the right rein; the instructor even split us up (there was a half-dozen in the lesson) so that we made two cycling groups of three at opposite ends, passing each other in the center. Round and round and bloody round we went, making the adjustments that were suggested (shouted) from the ground, and when it came time to dismount, we all wobbled on our thoroughly jellied legs, and if we'd gotten one correct circle out of it, then there was cause for celebration.

Notice I said "correct." Not perfect. That's where the madness of horseback riding is different from the insanity of codependency, which knows nothing of correctness, only per-fection. If one were behaving *correctly* in a relationship, then the lunacy of codependence wouldn't even get a chance to put its feet under the table. Correctness in this case has to do with balance, with a healthy give-and-take, and a blend of reliance and inde-pendence. In codependency, those involved become dependent on each other's dependence: in my case, I needed to be needed, and in order to keep that state in play, I took responsibility over and above the call of duty. If I didn't do enough, more than enough, then the relationship would be over. If I was perfect, then the relationship would be, too.

I behaved incorrectly in order to mitigate incorrect behav-ior, and at first, it was fine, because I thought I was creating lasting solutions; instead, I was putting a band-aid on a broken leg. I sustained a level of fear and anxiety that gradually became detrimental to my health and well-being, which had not only to do with my reactions to his actions and choices, but also with my insistence on solving problems that were coming thicker and faster as the years went on.

Eventually my need to be "perfect" began to turn into a need to be "correct"—even though I maybe didn't understand it at the time.

In one private riding lesson (I was the only student), I worked Joxer, my assigned horse, in figures of eight for thirty-five minutes. Over and over. In walk. Not trot, not canter, but slow, steady walk. The purpose of this exercise was for me to improve what are called "the aids"—specific signals conveyed via the rider's seat and legs and through the reins that tell the horse what the rider would like him to do. In the figure of eight, I was persuading Joxer to flex and bend, that is, to become supple through his neck and body as we went around the curves.

Again and again we changed direction in the center of the figure of eight, from the left to the right and back again, with me using my seat and my legs to encourage the bending and flexing I was informed I desired. When it was correct, there was no mistake: Joxer's head dropped down so that his neck was a straight line from his back to his withers to his nose; I could see a hint of his inside eye, meaning he was looking in the proper direction; I could feel his footfalls, stepping effortlessly. I knew what to shoot for, and doing this one thing, this figure of eight—over and over, with varying degrees of success—was deeply satisfying: slowly but surely, I was getting better at asking for what I wanted, gently and assertively, and the result was immediate.

I used to pay all our household bills, over and over. Rent, electric, gas, landline, both cell phones. I would keep track of the figures, write them on a post-it note, and hand it over to my husband. The post-it note would go missing, which wasn't a problem, because even if I hadn't written down the figures anywhere else, you can rest assured I kept a running tally in my head.

I would do this, again and again, because we were a couple, and what if one month *I* couldn't meet *my* responsibilities? I certainly hoped that I could rely on him to cover for me! If he couldn't pay half the bills, it wasn't a big deal, because next month it would all be fine. He'd find a new job and it would be better, he'd be happy in the work, the people would be less difficult, and he'd start to contribute. Next month, everything would change.

It didn't, despite my attempts to be gentle and assertive. As I continued to do this month after month, the notion that I could even suffer so much as a cold became impossible. I had to work through the slightest sniffle or else we'd start falling behind. I hustled to keep us on track, and it became such an ingrained habit I didn't notice how desperate and resentful I was becoming.

The first twenty-meter circles in a lesson are always pretty rough: the horse is testing you, to see how serious you are about the whole hour ahead, much less that first circle. With Cathal, for example, he really doesn't think I'm serious when I get up there on his back, even though I certainly am, and am certainly demonstrating it. If we are riding outside in the lower arena, he uses the walk through the parking lot and around the bend to start working out how he is going to get me to back off, to just chill, and let him do what he wants. *Surely,* he's likely thinking, *by the time we get there, she'll be happy to be sitting up here, chatting with her friends, enjoying the fresh air. Then I can enjoy hanging out with my friends, and maybe get to lick Spuddie's nose.*

Cathal is a sociable sort. He is a cob, which is a type of horse rather than a breed: he is stocky and sturdy, and barn lore has it that he used to pull a cart before he began life as a school horse. He halts like a boss, no doubt a nod to his former employment, but he is all over the joint when he starts a lesson. Early in his second career, Cathal was mainly ridden by youngsters who he dragged around the arena due to a lack of strength in their legs and seat; he'd gotten used to taking the piss and getting away with it. About ten minutes into every lesson, without fail, on the first circle, he would begin to balk, and unless I caught it (and he knows when I'm not going to, because sometimes, he is right, I do just want to sit up there and chat with my friends) he would stop dead, causing a pile-up behind us, and a spate of howling from the instructor on the ground.

A rider learns not to take hollering personally. The instructor shouts primarily to 1) be heard by the group and 2) do her job, which is to remind the rider of what *she's* supposed to be doing: she's supposed to keep her legs firmly in contact with the horse to get him moving forward, with the outside leg behind the girth so she can bend the horse around the inside leg (which is on the girth); she should be looking up and around the circle (if that's the figure she's meant to be riding), making sure not to drop her inside hand, always bending, bending, bending the horse to the inside, hands still, bending, bending, bending, bending.

You put on that inside leg to encourage the horse to bend his body *around* it; meanwhile, you try desperately not to yank on the inside rein so that horse is looking inward, because even though that's where he's *supposed* to be looking, yanking is the incorrect way to get him to do it. In fact, yanking makes things worse, as it encourages the back end of the horse to swing out and all of a sudden you're practically going sideways. So you increase the pressure from the outside leg to bring the hindquarters back into alignment, and shift your body's center just a little bit to further encourage that bend, and you try on top of all of this to ride your own circle and not just blindly allow your horse to follow the horse and rider in front of you, because the leader may be a horse that likes to start cutting in, making the circle smaller so he's done with it more quickly.

Also, you have to somehow manage not only to keep your hands up (reasonably up, not up around your ears, but not down in your lap, either) and your heels down (with the stirrup on the ball of your foot) and your toes pointing in, shoulders relaxed and down, chin somewhere between not too up and not too down, neck tucked back into your collar, all without worrying about the horse, because why would you worry about the horse if you're doing all the things you're meant to be doing, correctly?

Over and over and over.

Written out like this, it all sounds entirely bat-shit insane.

How did you get here?

If you were me, then one day you woke up and decided that you needed to be around horses. It was the proverbial bolt from the blue. You'd never even touched a horse in the whole of your life. There was that pony at the birthday party of a kindergarten pal, which was, like, over forty years ago. Maybe, every once in a while, you sidled up to the carriage horses that lined the south side of Central Park, but that was the extent of it.

So you bought books about them and you looked for a "horse place" that was nearby so you could maybe go look at them, in real life, and try the "whispering" and whatnot you'd read about. You attended a horse show in some random field that boasted large horse trailers, a perfectly assembled ring for jumping, and a fortune-teller in a caravan. (There were more people queuing for the tarot card readings than were watching the jumping.) As you leaned on the fence, a woman standing nearby struck up a conversation and proceeded to tell you everything you wanted to hear: that she started late in life, that she'd lost almost thirty pounds, that she was jumping now.

It didn't go away, this thought, this need, this want. A year or two later, you met a woman who had her own horse, so you got to ride for the first time, and you realized you hadn't the first notion of what you were doing despite all those books. You fell on your bum and limped for two weeks. Then, over the course of the next year or so, your marriage began to implode, so you decided to forget about the nutty horseback-riding-notion. But you didn't really. It wouldn't let you.

That idea of horses wouldn't go away. So, three months and four days after I left my marriage for good, I booked myself a real horseback-riding lesson.

The wee girls circled round and round, their legs pounding the sides of their ponies, and I was feeling breathless.

As excited as I was to take my first proper riding lesson, I realized I would actually have to be *on* a horse to take it, and God, they were big, weren't they? I watched those kids flying around the ring and felt increasingly fluttery and anxious. As little as I knew about horses, I knew this anxiety was a bad thing. I was already feeling under the weather: I had a headache as well as a scratchy throat, which was exacerbated by the unexpected heat of the autumnal day that had turned the Number 63 bus into a trundling sun trap...I could always come back another time.

No, I couldn't come back another time. I'd spent the entire week, in the run-up to this day, talking about it to the girls at work. The day I'd finally Googled "equestrian centers in Dublin," I saw: horse statues on a house on the coast road that I'd never seen before; a horse trailer; an *actual* horse; and on the way home from work, my iPod opened the evening's commute with "Land" from Patti Smith's *Horses*.

Okay, *okay*. I *got* it.

So, I'd made it to the horse place. I walked up a long, long road to a steep, steep hill. I didn't know where anything was, I didn't know who to make myself known to—I needed a helmet, I knew that much. I wandered around the arenas and paddocks; I was an hour early, thanks to the bus. I was intimidated by the thoughtless ease with which a clutch of girls in hard hats inhabited the entrance to what was surely the main barn. I couldn't go near them; I felt like I didn't have the right.

I drifted over to the door of the inside ring. There were eight girls riding ponies and one women standing in the middle, yelling. Dirt flew from beneath hooves as the last girl stopped going fast (Were they "cantering"? I wondered) and the woman in the middle told them all to line up at "K," one of the random letters nailed to the walls. Parents hung out in front of the half-doors, chatting amongst themselves and happily complimenting their daughters as they sped past. These kids were now leaping over obstacles. Jesus God. I drifted away.

Then an older bunch of riders came back from somewhere, rode into the ring, and everyone slipped effortlessly out of their saddles to the ground. The horses were led out and taken to the barn, voices were raised simply to be audible, and I backed away from the group—I really needed that helmet. I found a door labeled "Office" and entered. There was a guy sitting behind a desk who seemed to be in charge, so I told him my name, and he said, "You're late."

A helmet, stinking with hours and hours of strangers' sweat, was jammed on my head, and I was instructed to go back to the indoor arena, and I did, and there the teacher asked me who I was and had I done much riding, and I told her my name, and said none, and she told me to get up on a black horse, and I did, and she showed me how to hold the reins, and I held them, and she told us all to walk on, and—

And the horse took one step, and I thought to myself, *Fuck*, and he took another and I thought, *Fucking hell get me the fuck offa this fucking*—and another step and another, and then I was no longer a human woman but a sack of frozen potatoes sporting a fetid black hat.

I didn't even know the black horse's name. How were we supposed to bond?

I could hear myself breathing, air whistling in and out of my nose. I heard a voice shouting, but it wasn't language: it sounded like short, sharp raps. There was a sensation that it was

30

the same series of sounds over and over: rap rap rap. The other people on horses in the arena understood and were obviously responding to these sounds, because one minute, we were going in one direction, and then we weren't: we were threading our way from one corner of the arena to the other and going the opposite way...and I'd yet to fall off.

And with maybe fifteen minutes to go (I didn't dare glance at my watch, because if I moved my hands, or wavered in my unstinting regard of the back of the horse's head, something bad would happen) it occurred to me to maybe relax my stiffened legs a little, like, maybe even grip the sides of the horse, with my calves? Was this is a good idea? I did it, and I immediately stopped hyperventilating. The teacher wasn't bothered that I wouldn't do anything but walk ("Sue, want to give the trot a go?" "No."), and I sensed that my lessonmates were still where they were meant to be, on the backs of their horses, not writhing around on the ground clutching shattered limbs...and I relaxed.

That relaxation, and the action of my calves tightening, as well as this intuitive (commonsensical!) decision, resulted in a somewhat straighter spine. I sat better, and that enabled me to hazard a look around, and to drop my elbows a little, although my arms were so tense you could have shattered concrete blocks on them, and my hands were so thoroughly clenched on the reins I was sure I'd broken all my finger bones.

Suddenly, the staccato rap-rap sounds became language: "Turn in and give them all a big pat.... Feet out of the stirrups... swing your leg around...drop down," and I was back on the ground. I leaned against my soon-to-be-erstwhile trusty steed and noticed a nametag on the horse's bridle.

"Mercury," I whispered in his ear, "Mercury! You are great!" Mercury snorted and dropped his head, stretched out his neck, and then brought his face back up, one eye looking directly into mine.

I walked down the steep hill to the long road to the bus stop, my hair having fully absorbed, via the helmet, the honest sweat of women like me—women who have ridden a horse. I no longer had even the smallest trace of flu, or headache, or sore throat, or a single critical thought about what I'd just done. Swaggering like a cowboy (there's a reason they walk like that), all I thought was, *I did it, I did it, I did it!*

I'm fairly sure I've never been so delighted in my entire life.

I was never as delighted as when I was in love. I loved being in love. Or I was in love with the idea of love. Or I loved the stories I made up whenever I had a crush on someone. I was happy enough to dream up possibilities despite the probabilities before me: this person didn't seem entirely broken up from his partner; that one professed he was too damaged to be in a relationship and yet kept calling; another was only available on his terms, and never when I wanted him to be. The uncertainty was exciting, and the heartbreak inevitable.

So when I fell for horses, I went all in, and after two years in the saddle, I reckoned I was ready to take the next step.

In a private lesson with Roisin, my instructor, I told her I was thinking about starting to look for a horse. Of my own.

Horse people tended to think you were crazy if you didn't have your own horse, because look at all the money you'd save! (I still haven't quite figured that claim out yet. I mean, I actually did do the math, and it doesn't really work that way—unless we're talking about some kind of emotional economics.) And they really thought you were nuts if you paid to ride someone else's horse four times a week, which I was doing at the time.

I said to Roisin, "I'm definitely not getting a mare."

"Why not?"

Uh. I blushed and tried to remember what I'd read about female horses. "They're moody, right? And difficult? Although, I did hear someone say that a mare will take better care of you, like, correct herself to help when you're jumping, more than a gelding would."

"Mares can be moody," Roisin agreed.

"Definitely," I responded.

"But once you get them on your side, a mare will be really loyal."

"Oh, I'd like that," I said decisively. "A mare might be good, then."

"But a good gelding can be more even-tempered," Roisin continued. "Depending on what age he is, of course."

Of course. And the conversation went on, in the kind of indirect and slightly convoluted, yet unequivocal way that horse people have of explaining things—that one idea is complete bullshit...but then there are certain cases in which it would not be.

This leads to the absolute fact that the right horse for me is the right horse for me, and that's all there is to it.

The next week, I said to Roisin, "I'm definitely not getting a horse that hasn't had lesson experience."

This statement was treated in much the same way as my declaration the week before.

"What do you mean?" She looked up at me as I adjusted my stirrups.

"I mean..." I reached down to tighten the girth and buy some time. "I need one that knows how to behave in the ring with other horses...that won't freak out or something?" My statement somehow sounded like a question.

"Do you mean you wouldn't take a horse that's only hunted?" she called across the arena as she laid out some poles for me to trot over.

"Yeah!" I began to walk my day's mount around as a bit of a warm-up.

"But a horse that hunts likes to jump, and you want a jumper, don't you?"

Didn't I? Because I liked to jump?

I finally admitted, aloud, "Okay, look, I really don't know what I'm talking about."

I didn't. I didn't know what I was talking about. I didn't know anything about a horse's care and feeding, I didn't know anything about what to do if he got sick. I didn't know how long to turn him out or if I should turn him out, and what I would do if I couldn't get to the barn to turn him out. I now knew how to tack the horse and get on his back, and do other horse-related stuff for sixty minutes, but the whole rest of it, what went on in the twenty-three other hours of the day when I was not there, was a riddle wrapped in a saddle pad inside a mystery.

The biggest mystery was all this "right horse" business. Horse people didn't mess around. They didn't use any more words than were absolutely necessary. If they believed in it enough to talk about it, then it must be true. My knee-jerk reaction was cynicism (this "right horse" business sounded fanciful, like a fairy tale) and I couldn't countenance it...because of course, I wanted to countenance it desperately. *I wanted there to be the right horse for me.* I wanted to walk into a stable yard and see him or her from across the dusty paddock and have my heart leap into my throat. I wanted to get up there and know, just as, or even before, my bum hit the saddle, that this horse was *the one*. I wanted the clouds to part, I wanted the sun to pour down on me and my four-legged BFF as if flowing out of a divine spigot. I wanted a celestial chorus to burst into song as we cantered, in slow motion, to the crest of a hill that overlooked the sea.

Except there was all the stuff that had to do with hay and farriers and blankets and clipping and lameness and God knows. I didn't know any of this stuff, and I didn't know if I'd ever be able to learn it all.

In anticipation of my second lesson, I'd been thinking about trotting all week. Every single day. Waiting for the bus, walking to get a salad at lunch, staring into the middle distance, bored, at work.

Some of the seemingly unintelligible sounds issuing from the mouth of the instructor from my first ride appeared to have been processed as knowledge in the far reaches of my brain. Talking to a couple of girls at work who had ridden before, I realized that I had, in fact, learned something as I walked along on Mercury—in theory, at least. One of my coworkers showed me what "rising trot" was meant to look like, alternately standing and sitting in her office chair; another said something about "heels down" and "leg on the girth." I had figured that part out already! Excellent.

I thought about how to hold the reins properly, with my pinkie finger closed, how to sit in the saddle without curling up in a defensive ball (not unlike the fetal position, which, I understand, is instinctive on horseback), of sitting then rising, sitting, rising, sitting, rising, around and around in a big circle, sitting rising sitting rising as the horse trotted, which would be faster than a walk. This seemed daunting, like it was too much to ask, too soon...but I was going to do it.

My second Saturday at the barn, I knew what to do. I changed into my dressy boots that went up my leg; I'd need proper riding boots if I kept this up. I hung my backpack on the pegs near the bathroom. I chose a helmet, wincing inwardly at the prospect of putting it on; I'd need one of these too, if I stuck with this riding thing. I held off putting it on my head, hooking the chinstrap closed so I could dangle the hat from my hand, and I wondered if that was how actual horse people—the ones who knew what they were doing—carried them. I ventured over to the arena, the little girls going round and round, and I watched for a while, and tried to learn.

Yep, there was that heel thing that I had been thinking about; it seemed to allow the girls to rise up and down from the saddle with a minimum of effort while trotting. The instructor's directions made more sense to me standing on the earth than they had sitting up on the horse's back, and I guessed that those random letters on the walls were important, because she kept calling them out, and then the girl in front would do something, like go in a different direction, and everyone else would trot along and follow. After they'd briskly traversed the arena at an angle ("Change the rein on the long diagonal from M to K!") the lead girl started cantering. I couldn't tell how she'd done it: one minute she was trotting, up down up down, and then the next she was going faster, in a lovely rocking-horse movement. It looked beautiful, like real horseback riding, but it also scared the living daylights out of me. What if the instructor tried to make me do *that*? I wasn't ready—no way. My heart started beating as fast as it had the week before, and all my preparation went out the window.

The next girl started to trot, did the invisible thing that made the horse canter, and I stepped away from the doors, feeling panicked. I glanced toward the barn. The doorway was empty. I walked up the rise and went in.

It was dark, and it stank, and the concrete floor was littered with hay and plops of poo. I smelled horses and horse piss,

36

and suddenly I knew that if I was a Viking spirit rising from its burning bark, all of this would be redolent of Valhalla.

The horses watched me—two legs, food-bearing?—and I greeted them all. Each one was so different: the dark bay, the light bay, the one that was straight-up brown, the one that was chestnut, some curious, some not bothered, some ears pricked forward, some laid back. I moved along, patting, stroking, exchanging breath with a big guy that was interested enough to want to know me a little better. I wandered down the aisle, from stall to stall, saying hello, alone, no one telling me to stop, no one telling me it wasn't allowed, no one telling me that I didn't belong. They seemed to like me, the horses, and I calmed down.

I figured my lesson, trotting and all, was going to be okay—until I found myself back in the arena, where I was told to take "Argo." All week, I'd been mentally practicing on Mercury. This wasn't going to plan.

A woman smiled at me from across the arena and waved.

Holy shit. She was standing beside a huge chestnut, whose head hovered well above hers. Was this Argo? *My* Argo? Flanked by the other horses from the lesson that was about to begin, he stood much taller than they, and his big head kept swinging around, taking in the fuss and noise of riders exiting and entering the ring.

I walked up to them. "Argo?" I asked, a little hopeful that I was mistaken as the woman handed me his reins. She nodded. "He's big," I said, breathless all over again.

"Oh, he's lovely," she replied, feeding him Polo Mints.

"Big." I stared at the bottom of his neck, then the top of his shoulder—shoulder? Was it called a shoulder on a horse? Whatever it was, that feature of the horse's anatomy was slightly above my eye level.

I stood five feet, nine inches tall. Crap.

"He's a beautiful guy," the woman crooned, giving him one more stroke down the flash of white on his face before wishing me a good lesson and departing. I struggled to unhunch my shoulders, hell, my whole body, as she left me alone in charge of this massive beast.

I looked into the eye closest to me.

Argo turned his gigantic head, and rubbed it up and down my entire torso.

"Hey!" I said with a laugh, bracing myself, stroking a hand down his neck. He rubbed and rubbed, and I whispered nonsense in the general direction of his left ear. A couple of the books I had read said a horse was showing a lack of respect when he "got in your space" like Argo was, uninvited, but in that moment, I decided what the books said was total nonsense. I was delighted—ecstatic!—as he briefly rested his forehead on my chest, and we both breathed together.

The same instructor from the previous week, who reintroduced herself as Niamh, greeted me as she set a block of plastic at my feet, presumably to get me closer to giant Argo's saddle. I stepped up onto it and was not much higher off the ground than I'd been before.

"Can I turn it the other way? Onto the short end?" I asked. Who knew what was allowed or not?

"You can, of course." Niamh flipped it up as she cast an eye around the arena to make sure all was well with the other students and their mounts. I tried to ignore the fact that most of them were on already.

I stepped up onto the short end of the block—it was less secure, but I coped with the wobble because I was that much closer to the top of the horse. I tried to raise my left foot up into the stirrup; I couldn't even get my toe into it. I had seen someone else messing with the strap that held it, so I lengthened the piece of leather a notch. I tried again; lowered it some more. I ended up putting my hand under my thigh to lift my leg, finally wedging my foot in the iron—it was like my leg and foot were completely numb and couldn't function on their own. I wiggled the stirrup around until it was under the ball of my foot.

"All right?" Niamh asked.

"Almost," I muttered. I bounced on my right leg, the block started rocking, and I threw myself sideways and up, my right arm draped all the way over the saddle, my right hand grabbing onto something on the other side, my left hand clenched onto the front, which curved over Argo's neck without laying flush against it. I dragged my torso up until my leg straightened, threw my right leg over, and then I was *up there*, sitting on top of this gigantic animal.

Niamh helped me sort the reins. "Next time, I'll get you to hold onto these as well."

Oh, shit, what? How was I going to manage that?

I didn't have time to dwell on this new development. The lesson began. This time, I was able to hear and understand Niamh's words: advice about keeping my heels down, and something about my hands—that I should keep them down, too, I thought, but wasn't sure. As we walked the horses around, she told us to do things when we reached different letters on the walls—change direction on the diagonal line across the arena from F to H, walk in a circle at C. They went by me in a blur: *AKEHCMBF.* Niamh gave us a mnemonic to remember their order: *All King Edward's Horses Carry Many Brave Fools.* I promptly forgot it, as much of my attention was focused on remembering to breathe.

I felt less and less wobbly as Argo and I went along. I started moving with the horse as he walked: "One-two-three-four, one-two-three-four!" Niamh shouted from the ground. I had no idea why in the world she was counting. She told the rider who was first in the line of horses moving around the perimeter of the arena to start trotting, and to do so until she reached the end of the line. Somehow, some way, I was able to watch that woman trot and still manage to stay in the saddle.

The next rider, now at the front of the line, went trotting around until she came to the back, where she got the horse (somehow) to return to a walk. Oh my God...I hadn't thought about *stopping* the trot! How was I going to do *that*?

"Okay, Sue, want to trot?" Niamh hollered.

"Yes..." I called back, rather unconvincingly.

I took a breath.

I squeezed my legs.

Argo took one big step, then another big step, and started to build up steam.

I rose in the stirrups and lowered back down.

We trotted. We trotted around the arena with Niamh now barking, "One-two, one-two, one-two, one-two!" and telling me to do things that I hadn't a hope of doing—something about my chin and looking where I was going—and I kept going up and down, and Argo kept going forward, and then we were at the back of the line, and Niamh instructed, "Sit back, hands down, sit back!" and Argo stopped trotting and started walking.

And I was hopelessly and blissfully hooked.

I used to get a buzz of sorts from trying to control someone else. It was an addiction in its own right, something I actively chased. That rush of attraction to someone not in the least bit appropriate had always been unutterably exciting, even if I knew better. I was a pro at ignoring the little voice inside—actually, I either didn't have one of those or it was so infinitesimal that there was no way it could be heard. I was too busy to hear anything that wasn't a bellow, too busy working loony hours, and having a thousand side projects, and looking for everything I needed to make me feel good about myself, outside of myself. Sure, I went to therapy, and I worked very hard on my "journey," but the key, the main hook, eluded my comprehension. I really didn't know what was wrong with me. Part of me didn't really want to know.

In common parlance, this is known as denial.

At the end of the nineties, I decided it was all Manhattan's fault. If it wasn't so hard to live there, so exhausting, so expensive, such a relentless grind, then I would absolutely have the kind of life I wanted. You could tune out the noise, but you couldn't tune out the underlying hum of desperation, a composition of tones: impatience, waiting for a big break; frustration, realizing you had to stay in the job you hated or you'd never be able to buy own your own apartment, much less a place up the river, like Dobb's Ferry—holy God, the prices! I was doing so much all at once: working full-time as a magazine designer; working part-time with an independent, unfunded theatre company; writing short films and then producing them. I had those crushes that went pear-shaped, dates that went nowhere, and it took a lot for me to let either go, because who knew when I'd ever meet somebody else? Stupid city, making me lonely and miserable. I just knew that if I left New York, everything would come together. It would work out. All I needed was a new place to be.

I moved to Ireland in 1998. I applied to do a Masters in Philosophy at Trinity College, Dublin, got in, and managed to get the whole thing organized in a little over four months.

I, and many of the people I knew in Manhattan, had Irish roots. Everyone was certain that I'd have a great time, back in "the homeland." But growing up, we never talked about Ireland in my house, despite my father's mother having emigrated from Limerick City in the twenties. She never spoke of her native country, not even to my dad. It may have been because the Ireland of her childhood was a grim, depressing site of unsettled politics and impoverishment. I don't think she could bear to speak of it: for better or worse, she was never going home again. There was nothing to say.

So really, the extent of my Irishness was dotting my face with green magic marker ("freckles") on the seventeenth of March each year. I did visit the country once in 1996, although I don't remember making a conscious decision to do so. I think I picked up the *Irish Echo*, maybe, saw ads for cheap flights, and suddenly there were airline tickets in my mailbox. I bought a guidebook, and off I went.

What I do remember, clearly, is disembarking the plane. I remember the chill of the western Ireland country air, the dampness that seemed to lay itself on my face like a cool cloth, and the smell, the smell of the earth, and the smell of something burning, like logs in a hearth, but not: something that smelled warm and welcoming. I remember figuring out how to get to the lake that I imagined was the site of pleasant outings taken by my paternal "grandfamily." I remember getting off a bus, walking down a lane, and hearing nothing but the sound of my feet on the tar macadam, the sound of my breath, and the buzzing of a bumblebee. I had been in the middle of the madness of Manhattan less than twenty-four hours before; in that moment in Ireland I felt so present. I was the only creature on the road, I was alone in a foreign country, not entirely sure I knew where I was headed or if this was the road that was going to take me where I wanted to go, and yet it didn't occur to me to be worried or afraid.

It also didn't occur to me to be afraid of the actual move two years later until it was, helpfully, far too late. All the excitement and bustle and planning and packing was done. There I was, occupying seat 22D on flight EI108, sitting down with nothing to do for hours and hours, except maybe indulge in a well-deserved nap...my eyes flew open and I stared at the overhead light and thought: *What have I done?*

Was I completely out of my mind? I'd left an excellent job with a future working as a publications designer, a great living space I was renting from a pal, and a social network that had taken sixteen years to build. I was going back to college, for crying out loud, to get a Masters I didn't need, so I could live in a country that I had been to only twice and a city that I'd spent almost no time in (and was, in fact, rather happy to vacate both times I'd visited).

I had a life. And I had packed it all up, stored away the friendships, shelved the business connections, had one last weird New York date (a hike with a guy, and some friends of his, up a spur of the Appalachian Trail that went on, and on, for, like, six hours), and told everyone I was just going for a year, just one year abroad.

Even as I said it, over and over, I knew it was a lie. Or perhaps it was simply a function of my denial: If Ireland didn't "make" me happy, then I would move back to New York, refreshed, and able to take on the city again. But...I absolutely did not want to have to go back. I'd read so many accounts by expatriates, living in a variety of countries, the ones who had "left it all behind" and "made a new life" somewhere else, a place that was not where they'd started out—and I wanted to be just like them. I wanted the thrill, the extraordinarily difficult *thrill* of not knowing what was going to come next; the buzz of having to call upon all my skills to manage the unfamiliarity, the slight dis-ease of not knowing how things worked, the excitement of figuring out how to cope in strange circumstances. The harder I pushed myself the better, because I would prove I was able, no matter what.

Niamh walked into the barn with the evening's list of equine allotment. I'd been thinking—but not in front of Argo—that it had been at least twenty weeks now...and seven of them riding twice a week...and that maybe I ought to...

"You want to have a go on somebody else tonight?" Niamh asked. She looked at me, giving me room to make the decision, but I could see, in her eyes, that it was time for me to try a different horse.

"Should I?" I asked in return, unwilling to take the leap all by myself.

"If you want to," she replied, not giving an inch, her gaze becoming slightly impatient. There were other riders to see to; we didn't have all night.

"Yeah," I said, breathing out. "Yeah, okay."

"Take Delilah."

I had already noticed Delilah, a beautiful dark bay, one of only three mares in the barn.

"Hey, Delilah." I went into her stall, undid the throatlatch of her bridle, unwrapped the reins that were secured there, did up the throatlatch again, and led her out.

I had bonded with Argo—or he with me, or both—without much effort. Geldings are like that. Mares, however...well, I'd read about mares.

We stood in the indoor, and I waited to mount; despite all the progress I'd made, I still couldn't do it by myself.

Delilah wasn't giving me much; she just stood there. Once, in the barn, maybe a month before, I'd given her a good scratch on the withers, and she'd reached over and started mouthing at my shoulder, grooming me in return. I tried this again.

Nothing doing.

Niamh brought the mounting block over and held the offside of the saddle as I put my foot in the stirrup and after a few preparatory hops, hauled myself up. Once mounted, I made the first mistake of the evening. I thought she might like a little serenade, you know? A bit of a tune, and in fairness, how could anybody resist? Lowly, I intoned, "Why, why, why, Delil—"

She shot me a look over her left shoulder, ears pinned back.

"Sorry, Dee Dee." Whoops. She bared her teeth; she didn't like that, either.

It all went downhill from there. Delilah was narrower and, at first, more spritely than Argo. I struggled to find a rhythm, trotting with less grace than she preferred. She spooked when Niamh came to fetch my whip to give to somebody else, and then, when Delilah realized that I was sans crop, she proceeded to plod, to ignore my aids, to toss her head. Finally, she refused to trot at all.

Throughout this textbook display of mare bravado, I felt my embarrassment turn to frustration, which built into anger. By the end of the hour, I didn't want to give her a small pat, much less a big one. Once I dismounted, we stood side-by-side, silent, cold-shouldering one another.

By the time I got home, I felt bad for having blamed her entirely; she was simply dealing with the rider she was dealt. I had not been gracious in the end. Not even so much as a thank you in the form of a treat.

I was ashamed of myself. Why? Because Delilah couldn't do what I wanted us to do, and that was because I wasn't asking correctly. I looked back over the lesson: I was bouncing all over her back; I was hanging on the reins (because I was bouncing);

my aids weren't clear (due, again, to bounce). Her fault? Well, she was bouncy. But I needed to own the lack of balance in my seat. Plus, I gave up on her mid-lesson, and why she should do anything when I was not asking her to do anything? She wasn't a mind-reader.

The next morning, I booked myself a lesson for Thursday. And come Thursday, I approached that evening's instructor, Emily, in the parking lot. "Can I have Delilah tonight?" I asked as she closed the trunk of her car.

She looked surprised, if not shocked. Argo and I were famous for being a pair. "You can, of course," she replied. "Trying someone new?"

"I had her on Tuesday," I explained. "It didn't go well."

"Ah, Delilah," Emily said with a laugh, and we both turned and headed for the barn. "You didn't sing her that song, did you?"

I approached Delilah's stall, where she was standing with her back to the door. I felt a wave of remorse go straight through my heart.

"Delilah." She flicked an ear in my direction but stayed standing with her hindquarters facing out. "Delilah. Sorry. I'm sorry—I was frustrated, and you were sticking it to me, but—I'm just sorry. It was crap. I didn't even pat you, and I felt awful afterward...."

Somewhere, maybe at the second "sorry," the mare slowly shifted and swung around to face me. She ended my plea for forgiveness, putting her nose right up against mine, blowing gently, allowing me to breathe back. I felt pardoned, and even though that night's lesson was tough, it wasn't as bad as the one previous, and if it wasn't too bonkers, I liked to think she felt better about it, too.

The majority of equine literature takes great pains right from the get-go to explain the nature of the horse as a herd animal, and that in order to enter into the correct human-horse relationship, we must be the leaders. Many books say that this is where women fall down. Professional relaters from birth, we have no difficulty with the bonding part, the grooming and the treating and the whispering. Where we stumble is in the attitude of power: We want the horse to do what we want the horse to do, but what do we do when the horse won't do it?

I can be wishy-washy in leadership scenarios. I was, very much so, with Delilah, albeit in a grumpy, sulky way. I figured that she knew more than I did about this horseback-riding caper, since she was a horse and had been ridden for years, but it wasn't her job to be the creature ridden *and* the creature running the ride. Delilah would only do what I told her to do. The whole point of riding is to work with the horse to achieve a goal, not just sit there and hope she does the job for you.

Take Maverick, the fourth horse I was ever to ride in my life. Unlike any of my previous horses, he seemed perfectly content to engage in a power struggle, lesson after lesson after lesson. And I showed up for it every time. Even when I had four horses I could choose from, I routinely went back to him, and I'd be surprised when I found we hadn't made much progress. This was especially frustrating, because when we had a good hour, it was a really good hour. During the first few weeks that I rode him, I actually wrote this on my blog:

> I love Maverick! He's a gorgeous dun color, and he's
> feisty, playful, he kicks up a bit, he lets me know when
> I'm doing something he doesn't like, but he's willing,
> so willing, and he jumps like a dream. His canter—oh,
> his canter is just perfect. I've never felt so centered in

the canter, and during the last one, I lost my outside
stirrup, but he's so smooth, I just kept going, and it
was great.

None of my love letter was precisely incorrect...but I still
had a lot to learn where Maverick was concerned. He *was* gorgeous, and people who didn't know better, like parents of new
kids, sometimes thought he was my horse. They would come over
to tell me how handsome he was, and sometimes I'd pretend that
he *was* mine, and I'd smile and nod, and walk away with him at
my side, slowly, laconically, like a real horseperson.

But then there were the days when he wouldn't let me
bridle him, where I'd put the reins over his neck, the whole
shebang shaken out so everything—noseband, throatlatch, brow-
band—was going in the right direction as I held the cheek pieces
in the correct place and tried not to worry (much) about sliding
the bit into his mouth. All that would be fine. But then there was
the part where I had to get the top loop of the headstall over one
of his ears, then the other. For Maverick, both ears were a battle-
ground, and he'd throw his head, and I'd dance in place, feeling
like my arms were about to be dislocated from my shoulders. It
was war, every single time.

In winter, he'd be fizzy because it was cold out. In spring,
he was fresh because the weather was warming. I once said something to Roisin about how I was making progress with Maverick;
she shook her head and said, "No matter how much better you
get, Maverick is so tough mentally that he'll just come up with
some other way to torment you."

No one at the barn paid me any mind when I vented about
the gelding. They probably just wondered why I made myself
crazy trying to ride him. No, I thought, one day it would be perfect and I would have mastered this riding-Maverick thing, and I

was not giving up. He pushed me, and in turn I pushed myself, and that was good, because I was learning...right?

That's perfectly correct—except when it's not.

Another salient point that equine literature gets across is that horses are sentient biofeedback machines. They only give back what they receive. So, when I was getting more and more frustrated with Delilah, it could be argued that, as I went farther and farther down my I-suck-at-this rabbit hole, she simply responded to that information, and provided me with ample fuel for the fire. And if Maverick showed up, girded and ready for battle, whose fault was it that I kept choosing to engage?

I also struggled riding Charlie, particularly when trotting over poles. Trotting on Charlie was like being tossed upward—like I was lying in the middle of a sheet held by four people, one at each corner, and they were bouncing me up and down. There was a terrible weightlessness as I rose up out of the saddle, and it felt even worse going over poles. So bad was the feeling, in fact, I spaced out. I stopped paying attention, and just drifted off. As my mind wandered away from the job at hand, Charlie came to a dead stop. Right over the poles.

"Sue!" Emily hollered. "What are you doing? Trot! Trot!"

I kind of laughed, and shouted in return, "It was my fault, my fault!"

Because of course it was. Charlie knew I'd essentially just "disappeared," and he handled it the best way he knew: he stopped.

Right, so. In order not to drive my mount demented, I had to:

1) Establish boundaries.
2) Be assertive.
3) But also be patient (with myself and them).
4) Pay attention!

5) Work through difficulties and power struggles.
6) Admit when I'd been at fault.
7) Oh, and the physical stuff: Get a stronger leg and better balance and timing.

Each of these things, every single one (well, maybe not number 7), was something I could stand to do better in my life "on the ground," much less in the saddle, and definitely could have improved upon in my erstwhile marriage. Did I think that relating to a horse was going to be easier than relating to a human?

I did. I did think that.

I must have been nuts.

I returned to New York in the autumn of 1999 for a beloved friend's wedding, almost a year to the day since my move across the water. Finding myself on a certain stretch of an avenue in Manhattan, I suddenly thought about a guy I'd known who I thought might work nearby. At that very moment, there he was, waiting on the corner for the light to change. I called his name, we went for coffee, something clicked. A month later he rang, saying he was coming to Ireland, and a real romantic saga began, complete with sweeping soundtrack.

That visit was the beginning of a long-distance relationship. That guy was my future ex-husband.

I can't think of a better type of relationship for a codependent than an LDR. The separation! The drama! The longing telephone calls! The shitty telephone calls that throw the whole thing into question because someone says something contentious, and neither of you can see the other's reaction, and everything gets taken the wrong way (see: drama)! The dodgy emails that never quite live up to expectation! The elaborate reconstruction of The Relationship in periods of rest, each having retired to his or her own corners!

In my corner, I made up a whole story about The Relationship, which had almost no bearing on the reality of the situation. I would freak out when my space was "invaded," he would freak out when his was likewise, and yet I worked and worked and worked to make it work.

I immediately began to do everything in my power to control the situation. I was freelancing as a designer at the time—so I took off a month here and there in the first year and went back to New York. He didn't have email at the time—I set up an account for him. The phone bills were adding up—I bought him long-distance calling cards. I was ready to commit, so I did. I didn't really mind organizing his life because I was good at organizing things—and it was no big deal; he'd do everything himself after I did it the first time.

Right?

The first time I was told to canter in a circle, I suspected Emily was out of her mind. Why would she make us go fast in a shape that we had yet to trot properly? What good could possibly come of it? She asked me why I thought she'd have me canter in a circle, and I had no idea. I was on Delilah, and I still wasn't giving her the aid for canter in a way that she understood or accepted, and the whole thing was a nightmare. In addition to all the bits that I had to do when trotting in a circle—inside leg on the girth, outside leg behind the girth, looking where I was going—when cantering in a circle, I had to do all those things at a much faster pace, and also put a little bit of extra weight in the outside stirrup—but not too much. (Emily's answer as regards why? Apparently cantering in a circle is a standard element in a dressage test.)

The first time I successfully cantered in a circle, I felt as good as I did my very first ride on Mercury. Despite having thought it would require a huge change in what I was already doing, it really didn't—in fact, when cantering, I was more secure in that my butt was entirely seated, unlike the up-and-down of rising trot. All that was required was to sit deep and stay deep, a tiny change that yielded a new result.

The degrees of change in horseback riding may be as fine as those of codependency, but they fall on the healthy side of the fence. Or do they? The qualities in my personality that seemed to get me in endless trouble—poor boundaries, denial, and that reckless desire to chase the buzz—had the potential to get me into the same sort of difficulty, in a physically dangerous fashion, when I was on horseback as they did in my personal relationships.

To be honest, falling on any side of any fence is never a good idea.

CHAPTER THREE

FALLING

As soon as I started taking riding lessons, I began to wonder
when I would fall. I was neither so foolhardy as to believe I would
never fall, nor did I go chasing that first tumble simply to get it
over with. I knew it would happen; I just didn't know when, and
I wanted to be as prepared as possible for when it did. This was,
of course, pointless. There was no way I was going to control that
fall. There was no way that I was going to know it was coming.
And sure enough, when it happened, I didn't have a chance.

The thing about falling off a horse is that one second you're
up, the next, you're down. There's rarely anything in between.
The brain mostly draws a veil over the experience, choosing to
fast-forward from the moment the body begins to hurl through
space until it hits the dirt.

This is what happens with the big ones, anyway. There are
some instances in which an adjustment—a grab of mane, a twist
of knees, sitting back—can reverse what seems inevitable. Sometimes, you can't do anything to prevent the fall; all you see is a
blur of wall and ground and horse as you go down. I have saved
myself being unseated by a buck, I have managed to avoid getting
turfed off at a fence—and there have been plenty of times that I
haven't, with varying degrees of bang and bruise.

By 2002, I had been muttering about horses to myself for about a year, maybe longer. It transpired that I met Sorcha, a young woman who had just bought her first horse after having ridden on and off since childhood. When she realized that, while I was a newbie, I was as passionate about all subjects equine as she was, she invited me to come along to see her steed. She thought that we might go for a ride.

It occurred to me that a proper lesson might be best, since I'd never ridden a horse before in my life. But I'd been reading about horses avidly; this seemed like an excellent opportunity to put form into practice. I mean, how hard could it be? You're just sitting there, right? Plus, I'd read all kinds of heartwarming stories, all kinds of women-and-horses stories, and I felt certain that since I wanted this bonding-with-the-horse thing so badly, the horse would sense my need and take care of me.

Roaming around the barn with Sorcha, I was struck by how different all the animals were, one from the other, in terms of personality. There was one horse huddled back against the wall of his box stall, peering at us nervously through his long fore-lock; a majestic mare looked at us over her shoulder, and then, wriggling her bum and flicking her tail imperiously, proceeded to ignore us; the little gray who trotted up from the back of his stall and rubbed his face all over my chest. All of them, all different, and my friend's horse different still: long, leggy, and a beautiful dark browny-black color, with big, blinky eyes. He didn't have much interest in me; Sorcha was the center of his world. I felt a pang of yearning. As she did all manner of things with bridle and saddle, he didn't move a muscle, except to swing his massive head around, never taking his eyes off her. After leading him out to the front of the barn, she motioned to a mounting block, indicating I should get up there, put my foot in the stirrup, swing on board.

Seriously? I thought I was going to die.

I had never felt so unmoored in all my life. I was a million miles away from terra firma, the animal was lurching from side to side as Sorcha lead him around in a circle, and I felt completely dissociated from reality. My mind was straining for Mother Earth, leaving my body behind to cope as best it could. This was in no way similar to looking out from the observatory at the top of the Empire State Building, or standing on the Cliffs of Moher in County Clare, seven hundred feet above the crashing Atlantic. In those cases, you are so obviously far away from the ground that you don't think about the distance between you and the earth far below or the possibility of falling. It's like you can't take it personally: that yawning abyss exists, but it doesn't really have anything to do with you.

On the back of Sorcha's horse, I was just far enough away from and just close enough to my usual, comfortable position, standing on my own two feet, that I didn't know where the hell I was. I was in limbo. I didn't recognize anything. Trees, rocks, cobblestones, walls: they were all a blur of background as I focused, as if my life depended on it, on the back of that horse's head. The world looked utterly changed from my new perspective, perched in a saddle, and I realized that I didn't have a notion what to do. As I gripped the reins for dear life, I thought maybe going on a ride wasn't such a great idea after all.

Nevertheless, after I awkwardly slid off Sorcha's horse and back down to the blessed, blessed ground, I allowed myself to be led over to another mounting block, where a big gray horse, Silver, was waiting. Unlike the little gray in the barn who couldn't wait to get to me, this guy didn't give two damns; neither was I impressed, to be frank...and it all went downhill from there. We were joined by a teen who was going to take us out on a trail; she didn't seem to process the information that I hadn't had much experience with horses, and off we went, down a narrow, busy road toward the woods.

The hedges proved too much temptation for Silver, and I spent much of the first fifteen minutes hauling his head out of the bushes. The cars sped by, passing so closely my heart was in my throat. I yearned for a secluded dirt track, sure that once we were off in the countryside, this horseback-riding thing would become the exhilarating experience I had expected.

Nope.

No sooner had we turned off the main road and onto a less-frequented path than a boy-racer on a motorcycle buzzed us from behind. Silver went completely and totally mental (in retrospect, I think he shuffled around a bit and tossed his head in annoyance), and I was screaming, "Whoa! Whoa!" and our teen leader was screaming at the boy-racer, and Sorcha was trying to calm us all down. The boy-racer shouted and revved and gestured and eventually, eventually, we all moved on.

Then came the puddle. I'd love to call it a "water hazard," but it was, in fact, a puddle. A big one, and possibly a deep one, and we weren't supposed to ride straight through it, because who knew how deep it was and what was at the bottom of it. The teen and Sorcha got to the other side, and it looked easy, like walking around it, only on horseback, but when it was Silver's turn, he stopped dead at one end of the puddle. He seemed to, I don't know—need me to tell him what to do? I didn't know what to tell him to do. The teen leader shouted instructions to me, which, in a sudden state of panicked deafness, I couldn't comprehend. So Silver took the initiative and took off, and suddenly I was falling off backward, onto my ass.

When I say, "took off," I now know that he cantered a bit: ba dum, ba dum. But then, to my inexperienced mind and body, he felt like Secretariat, lunging for the wire in the Run for the

Roses. The landing was hard, and the small mercy was that I didn't actually land in that puddle.

I got back on. I had to climb up on a rock in order to board, but I got back on. We went on our walk through the woods, where I was miserable, on high alert, waiting for the next scary thing to happen, in between the waves of pain that radiated up from my bum. (I visited my doctor a week later: I had fractured my tailbone.) Sorcha proposed that we cut down a muddy hillside to get back to the barn when it became clear that I was struggling. I had absolutely no faith Silver would not slip or slide out from under me, so I got off and led him the rest of the way home. It was February; the wind was rising; the sun was sinking like a stone. All I wanted to do was go home and cry.

I didn't try horses again for years, until the desire built up to such a degree that I figured it was worth the risk. And given that experience, it is probably unsurprising that I liked the boundaries of the arena. Some riders find going around and around the same small, enclosed area mind-numbing, but I loved the tidy formality of it, the safety of it: there were walls that kept the horses in check; even if they spooked at something, they really hadn't anywhere to go. And despite (due to?) the unpredictability of the horse itself, the equine world was steeped in lists and rules, such as:

1) Pass other horses on the inside.
2) Yield to riders when leading a horse on foot.
3) Do not, on pain of death, run anywhere on the premises.
4) Always shut the gate to a field behind you.

So when someone said to me, in passing, that it takes seven falls to make a rider, my orderly heart leapt with joy.

I wanted to be a rider! I had never wanted anything quite
as much: not to be a wife, a graphic designer, or a journalist.
To be a rider meant that I'd be imbued with that mysterious
essence horse people all seemed to possess. I'd have a gaze that
was mostly turned inward, my mind only on horses and not the
outside world. Becoming a rider would also demonstrate that I
could, out of nowhere, from a thought, decide to learn something
about which I knew nothing. That I could learn it through all
manner of trial and error, and enjoy myself to a degree I hadn't
felt since...since ever.

If I had to fall on my ass seven times to have all that, well,
then, I really didn't feel it was too much to ask.

I decided to invalidate that first tumble off Silver; I wiped
the slate clean and started to keep count.

We were riding in the outdoor arena, and it was a beautiful evening: spring had sprung, the light was golden. There were six of
us: Charlie and his rider were first, then Maverick and his, then
myself and Delilah. Emily made us trot while holding the jumping position, which meant we were hovering above our saddles,
bums in the air, our weight in our heels to keep us balanced.
This was the posture we would assume when the horse jumped a
fence. I had a mane-grabbing habit I was trying to break, and as
we came around the corner nearest the parking lot, I was holding
the reins, and only the reins. I noticed that Charlie's ears were
perked up, and I saw him glance left, and then Maverick had a
look, too, and...was he slowing down?

Then there came a resounding crash.

Charlie and Maverick and Delilah all leapt right (Delilah
had the farthest to go without disappearing entirely up Mav's

behind), and I had a split-millisecond to keep my balance and sit down in the saddle...

But I was going down. I could feel it. I saw my left foot slip out of the stirrup. I saw under Delilah's neck and between the reins. And I saw two horse-and-rider pairs, stopped, frozen, the horrified look on the face of the girl directly behind me—and then bang on the top of my head, then smack on my lower back—dammit!

Emily checked me out. She led me and Delilah into the center of the arena. I sat on a mounting block; Delilah nudged my shoulder. "Not your fault," I said, patting her nose. Not her fault, not mine—the fault lay with the stupid jackass who tossed an empty wheelbarrow into an empty trailer: the great clattering noise that came out of nowhere and spooked the group.

Eventually, I got back on, and we continued.

Delilah and I jumped almost two feet that day, which at that stage was fairly significant.

The next day, every time I turned my head too quickly I felt like my brain was bouncing loose in my skull.

I fell. I finally fell.

My first fall.

The horse world lost its collective head in early 2009 when Professor David Nutt published a report claiming that taking ecstasy (MDMA) was no worse than horseback riding. The Bristol University academic, writing in the *Journal of Psychopharmacology*, sought to compare the class A drug with "equasy," or Equine Addiction Syndrome (a cheeky term he coined himself). He proposed—provocatively—that horseback riding be made illegal, as it inspired the same degree of harmful brain chemistry as does MDMA, and that as many deaths resulted on a yearly basis from both pursuits. Horse folk went mental, not so much, I think, because they were being compared to recreational drug users, but rather because the slightest notion that their beloved sport was in danger was enough to get everyone up in arms.

Speaking from his position as chairman of the Home Office Advisory Council on the Misuse of Drugs in the United Kingdom, you've got to wonder what Nutt thought he'd actually accomplish by making this comparison. Did he think a horse person would be surprised to learn that equestrian pursuits are as mind-blowing as being off your face at a rave?

Athletic activities produce endorphins, those endogenous opiates responsible for such states as "runner's high." There you are, stimulating yourself through exertive movement, and your hypothalamus, the link between your nervous system and your pituitary gland, starts putting out the call for endorphins in order to trick your body into feeling no pain. When the endorphins latch onto the opiate receptors designed just for them, the result is that exhilarated feeling that you can only get from exercise.

Oh, and from falling in love.

Endorphins are involved in keeping long-term relationships going strong: they're produced during sex and create that delicious glow that accompanies the post-coital wallow. (If Nutt had really wanted to freak people out, he might have worked this notion into his argument.) There's also adrenaline, and dopamine, and serotonin; all sorts of chemicals get shaken and stirred in our bodies when we're preparing that cocktail d'amour.

The thing about this endorphin business, however, is that the yearning actually comes after the experience. Or, in sporty terms, when we stop the aerobic exercise, it is our anaerobic state that produces the endogenous opiates. So the thing that keeps us carrying on isn't actually the thing itself, but the lack of the thing. When I am on the horse, my attention is on the horse;

it's only afterward that I receive the full mental and physical, and yes, emotional benefit of the experience. If I think about riding during the days I'm not doing it, it's because I can't wait to get back that feeling of being on the horse.

Yep, lots like falling in love. Those first, heady days of thrilling discovery and blocked serotonin are like nothing else in the world, and it is the body's way of deluding the mind into getting close enough to another person in order to start making enough of the bonding chemical, oxytocin, to ensure the continuance of the species. The magic of my Long Distance Relationship was the physical absence: there was stuff that happened when we were together, the good and the bad, and then there was the time apart, during which the yearning, on my part, certainly encouraged me to keep the thing going.

After I ran into him on the street, and we had coffee, I gave him my number, and, well, I flew back to Ireland. When I told the story my friends replied with sighs and eager questions. Would I see him again at Christmas? Did I think he would call? It was terribly exciting.

So when he rang to say he'd booked a ticket to Ireland, that he wanted to come over to celebrate his birthday, I naturally said he could stay with me, and we'd tour around the country. I intended to parade him round my pals, show him off. And I began conjuring up a fairy tale in which the time we would spend together would lead to us falling in love and...

And then I didn't know what. I had no intention of moving back to New York. Who knew what was going to transpire? I found *that* terribly exciting too, in the way moving to Dublin had been thrilling, a little bit scary. It was going to be an adventure, like something out of a romance novel.

It may be that the stories we tell ourselves help keep the oxytocin flowing: science is investigating the role the neurochemical plays in the "re-wiring" of our brains, and there's a theory that there are "scripts" in the brain that can be rewritten into new mental "texts"—*if* the information is actually the result of new experience, that is, and not a rehash of old patterns. When your stories don't really resemble reality and are being used, shall we say, to paper over the cracks, then they aren't helping at all, and may, in fact, be detrimental. Why? When the stories prove false, when the construction crumbles under the lies we've told ourselves, it's then that we hit the dirt, wondering how in the hell we got there, flat on our backs and shaken, and unsure as to how bad the damage is.

A burly chestnut, Dancer was the biggest horse in the school, and his quirks were legion: Once when I rode him, as soon as I was on, he immediately (and appropriately enough, given his name) began tangoing backward. I was still trying to get the length of the stirrup leathers right, and when I stopped fiddling, he stopped moving; I tried again, and he pranced back.

He was a tough customer, but Dancer jumped like a dream. I yipped with joy as we cleared a fence at the canter, his whole body collecting and rising beneath me. It felt like a *real* jump, like a *real* equestrian would take. I couldn't wait to go at that fence again.

Dancer was a bit slow in his transitions, but we eventually got a good canter up. We were passing all the other horses and riders who were in a line, waiting their turn, and we were almost around to the front, and—

Dancer kicked out at Mercury! There was plenty of room between the two horses, there was no reason for the behavior, other than Dancer being Dancer, but he bucked as he kicked, and sure enough, I felt it again: that slow, inexorable slide. This time I saw my right foot slipping out of the stirrup, and despite his massive height (roughly "eighteen hands" high or about seventy-two inches from the saddle to the ground), my fall was slow, and in a strange way, kind of easy—and then I was flat on my back, the reins still in my right hand.

That was it for Dancer: he was sent back to the stable, banished due to bad manners—and also because I wasn't a good enough rider (yet) to make sure, if one can make sure, he didn't go for somebody again.

My second fall. I maybe didn't feel quite so stupid as I did the first time, but I did feel like I could have done *something* to avoid eating dirt.

Projection is one of the ego's defense mechanisms. Projection off the back of a horse in front of a bunch of people is one of the worst ego trips imaginable.

Not that people laugh at you when you fall—they usually are incredibly concerned, with good reason. I've seen some falls that have, as an old dear would say, "put the heart across me." I saw one girl cartwheel over Charlie's head, so high up in the air it was unbelievable that she didn't break something. I saw another get turfed off by Ruby, and she fell on her head: the top of her head stayed put, but her neck and then her whole body did this twist to the side, and we all gasped.

People are stupendously kind after you fall off a horse; it's just that when you feel like you're the only one in the lesson who is always going flying, it starts to get embarrassing.

Psychological projection acts in much the same way, only you're tossing responsibility for your own feelings off the back of your high horse. You're up there because you've got this notion that all the chaos that's erupted around you isn't your fault. Or if it is, it's because you're very loving, very caring, very worried about someone, and you're busy picking up the slack. Say, for example, your significant other can't hold a job so you take care of all the bills. A psychologist might suggest that what may actually be the issue is that you yourself fear being unable to pay your own way. By projecting your partner's inability onto yourself, you have to work that much harder, proving to yourself that you can—that you don't have to depend on the vagaries of someone else's behavior.

But are we all that powerful? Can I essentially dump my shit on someone else and make him "be" the crap I don't want to be? Freud talks about a case in which a spouse is thinking about cheating on his partner, proceeds to unconsciously project his thoughts onto her, and then begins to believe that she's the one having an affair.

When you think about it, the degree to which someone doesn't want to face up to his or her own feelings is completely demented.

Over the course of my LDR, moments of clarity would shine through, and I would think, *I don't know that this is actually working out*—and, terrified that it *wasn't* actually going to work out, I would indulge in fantasies. In one of my favorites we had a Celtic handfasting ceremony at a holy well we'd found on the west coast of Ireland. A Druid priestess would unite us, the Irish Sea only a few yards away, pounding on the shore. There'd be a fiddle and maybe a flute, I'd have wellies on underneath a beautiful gown, all our friends would be there, and it would be the turning point, complete with flowers and cake. So romantic! Much nicer than admitting that I had, quite likely, lost my reason.

Reason would have stated that I was building this man up into something that he definitely was not; that I was not willing to be either the hero or the goat. In fact, if I could be more clear-sighted then I would realize that I was dumping both roles on him. The simple truth was that, while there were many good and interesting things about him, about me, and about us together, we were both, in our own ways, emotionally unhealthy.

Such a diagnosis is not the end of the world. Nobody's perfect, and that's what therapy is for—people are able to get over their crap every day. Every single day, someone is sitting in a chair across from someone else, many someones are sitting in a twelve-step room, others are talking with spiritual advisors, and something is shifting for them. They are having breakthroughs, epiphanies, and awakenings. The clouds part, and meaning and clarity descend, and the way is made open for a full and fulfilling life.

My solution was to marry projection with denial, because surely two defense mechanisms were better than one. Falling for someone who is not good for you, well, it doesn't make good sense, but it does make a sort of sense. This sense is the sort that blossoms when you manage to not hear anything that anyone on the outside of the relationship tells you, when you fail to absorb anything that you read in self-help books, despite recognizing a need for them, when you hang on to one or more fantasies for dear life, even though staying in the game is becoming danger-ous, emotionally or physically or both.

I kept showing up for him, for better or worse.

I kept showing up for the horses, too. There had been women who never returned to the barn once they'd fallen. Laura broke her hand. Martina damaged her rotator cuff. I imagine I'd scared off a few, with a couple of my plunges.

The falls started coming harder and faster, and I began to be less blasé. If anything, I felt worse when I came off (yet again), because I kept thinking, I must be better at this by now...aren't I?

I had been riding exclusively at my first barn for one year and seven months when I decided to try a different stable, one that was on my side of town, for a private lesson.

I felt like I was having an affair.

Hermes was a strong, well-built cob. He had been brought in from the field just before my lesson, and he took a moment at the open door of the covered arena, every time we passed, to call for the friends he'd left behind. He was not in the least bit interested in me, and I wasn't managing to engage his attention. He grudgingly trotted when I asked him to, and he refused to listen to my request for the canter at all, so the instructor waved a longe whip at him.

I got distracted by her whip. Hermes leaped to the left. I slid off to the right.

"You fell?" The instructor was incredulous.

You lashed the fucking whip at him, I thought. "Yeah, well," I said.

I had landed in a damp patch on the ground. Let's just say it was an aromatic bus ride home.

A couple of weeks later: same (new) barn, same horse, a group lesson this time, outside riding ring. A different instructor was busily chatting with some of her colleagues, leaving the riders to make their own decisions regarding rein changes and whatnot. I was once again trying to get Hermes to canter for me. The line of riders had halted at the M marker and would individually pick up canter between C and M before heading toward the fence, which was set up at B. (I could change barns but that crazy riding alphabet seemed to be following me.) We came around the corner and Hermes was motorbiking it, cutting it sharp/sharper/sharpest. I leaned on the outside stirrup, off-effing-balance, and started to feel the saddle slip and slip...I went down. I fell softly onto the sand, and stood right back up.

No biggie. Except that the instructor came over, shaking her head, gesturing at the saddle, now completely over on Hermes's offside.

"See that?" She put her hands on her hips and gestured at my horse and his gear, all askew. Everyone else, waiting for their turn to jump, stared.

Yes, I saw it. Cow. "Yeah," I said.

She proceeded to lecture me on proper lesson preparation as she released the girth and righted the saddle. I was so pissed off my anger practically vaulted me off the ground and back in the tack.

I was beneath her notice until we started to jump. She raised the rails on the fence to over two feet. "Hermes—" She hadn't even bothered to ask my name. "—you don't have to do this."

"I can do it," I responded.

We trotted. Hermes still wouldn't canter, not until we were a few strides away from the jump, anyway, but we took it perfectly.

Showed you, I thought. I certainly wouldn't be coming back to *this* place anymore. Falls three and four were the height of ignominy; though the new barn was nominally closer to home, the affair was over. I went back to where I'd started.

I didn't fall for Kilternan, my initial lesson barn, at first sight. Sure, I *liked* it right away, primarily because the place was laid back, the staff didn't mind me hanging around (sometimes for a full hour before my lesson), and nobody passed comment, even though I was dressed like a complete fool for the first few weeks, wearing jeans and those silly boots and a borrowed helmet. I did strive to get my look increasingly right: jodhpurs, paddock boots, new headgear. I toughened up, abandoned the myriad layers and woolly scarf I initially swathed myself in, riding in just a T-shirt.

Horse owners asked me to do things like mind their mounts while they ran to get a hoof pick or hold their offside stirrup while they got on. I was becoming known, even if it was for being the crazy woman who took two buses all the way from the other side of town, a million miles away.

In the case of this love affair, distance was not an issue. I was learning that if a place gave off the right vibe, then I should be careful not to muck it up. There was a world of chemistry between horse and rider, rider and instructor, between the riders within a group lesson, and indeed, between the horses and the instructors. I wouldn't ride Maverick when Angela was teaching the lesson. He adored her and always tried to show off, bucking more than usual, pelting for the perimeter after a jump, desperate to go fast, to show his favorite person what he was made of. When Emily was instructing us, Dancer would do everything in his power to stand by her. Once, we were waiting in the middle of the arena watching others take their turns over a jump, and when he heard Emily's voice behind him, he turned a full one-hundred-and-eighty degrees to face her.

That kind of chemistry took time to build, and I knew you didn't just throw it away. The miles of my commute meant nothing when measured against a place where I could find such a delicate balance of all the elements conducive to learning and enjoyment.

One Saturday, Niamh was off, and I almost started hyperventilating with fear that the unfamiliar woman, holding the clipboard on which the daily allotment of horses was kept, wouldn't assign me Argo, making me take somebody new, or worse, to my mind (even though it was essentially the same thing) that she'd give Argo to somebody else.

Oh, Argo. How I loved him. I hadn't imagined that anybody but me and Niamh and Argo himself knew about "us," but of course they did. Despite their taciturn exteriors, every human involved in some way with the running of a lesson barn knows exactly what's going on and who's doing what. They simply don't make a big deal out of it...unlike just about every other authority figure I've ever encountered in my life. Hence, I have more respect for them than I've had for every other authority figure I've ever encountered in my life.

I think—I know—that if Argo had submitted a report after each lesson, it would have gotten progressively less piqued as the weeks went by and the instruction started to sink in. Once my hands stopped flapping around and the rising trot began to settle more into my hips and abs than in my ankles and knees, he was a much happier horse. And by extension, I was a happier rider because "my" horse was happy. And all the other newbie riders were jealous, certain that my rapid ascendancy (such as it was, bless them all) had everything to do with Argo, and nothing to do with my own efforts. I guarded him jealously, and in turn, he wanted all my attention: Once, I was answering a question put to me by a lessonmate and so was talking to her around Argo's head. He took a step forward between us and started nodding vigorously, obstructing our line of sight and quite successfully interrupting our conversation. We had to laugh. It was adorable.

It wasn't all wine and Polo Mints: One lesson commingled the adult beginners with the advanced kids, and right away, it became clear to me that Argo was not pleased. Every time a pony passed by, first in trot, then in canter, he threw his head around, making faces, crowhopping, becoming so seriously vexed I had to get off him and finish on Delilah. I reckoned he didn't like the kids much, and he loathed the ponies, so the next time we all had to ride together, I was not happy, knowing that Argo was not going to be happy...and—due to that invisible communication of internal states that goes on between horse and rider—well, it wasn't one of our better hours.

There was no single event, no single hour that led to our parting of the ways. Just a notion, a stray thought, a growing feeling of confidence that caused me to wonder about maybe moving on and trying another horse. It happened in the blink of an eye—no big drama, no recriminations, nobody got hurt. I can't say I didn't look back, because I did: I always watched him whenever he was in my lesson under another rider, and I hung with him by his stall when he was feeling sociable. I did my best not to begrudge his new girlfriends their joy in his demonstrable affection.

Argo would always be my first.

I hadn't considered marriage something I'd "do." This was likely a form of denial, which ensured I wasn't disappointed if it never happened. The likelihood seemed pretty remote given that I was either obsessed with a crush that never came to anything or trying to shake off a persistent suitor I didn't like very much. When a relationship derailed before such promises were traded, it wasn't a big surprise. The chemistry wasn't right, or maybe it was in the beginning but then dissipated, or outright disappeared, in a matter of days.

The notion, then, that a handsome man with whom I was acquainted sufficiently, and with whom I'd had that delicious snap of attraction, was flying from New York to Ireland to see me was amazing.

"I'm due a fling," I said to my pals.

This could be the one! I said to myself.

"He must really fancy you!" my friends exclaimed.

70

"I guess," I responded with a schooled shrug, while inside acknowledging, He really must!

I prepared to throw myself into whatever came next.

There was a jump course set in the upper ring, and we were going to give it a go. I was on Delilah, and she clearly wasn't crazy about this particular arena: she found it hard to lift her feet out of the deep sand, and by extension, it was harder for me to keep my ass in the saddle at the canter. There were only three of us in the lesson; I was the only one to jump as the others opted out.

I came around to the sixth obstacle, a green-striped crossrail, and Niamh shouted encouragement. The sun was setting and the moment was absolutely cinematic: I was entirely in tune with Delilah, we were moving as one, and while I was consciously aware of the riding, the action, it did not need to be mediated or monitored in any way. We were perfectly lined up for the jump, I wasn't looking down at the fence, my attention was on myself, which freed Delilah to do what she needed to do—and then...Delilah slowed, and instead of keeping my seat and giving her a tap on the shoulder with my crop, I started to jump the fence for her. Too early, dammit! I knew it as soon as I was doing it, and when the mare actually *did* leap, my chest was at her ears and off I went, somewhat over her head and to the right.

Everybody in the lesson groaned. I jumped up, annoyed with myself.

Niamh said I would have gotten a ribbon anyway.

My fifth fall.

My fifth fall was a classic case of me not doing my job (staying balanced, looking up, hands forward, heels down) and trying to do Delilah's job—that is, physically throwing myself forward as if that would help her get us over the fence. It wasn't the first time I'd done it, either, only I'd managed to stay on in those instances.

In life, and in horseback riding, you start to create habits. The first time you do something, well, it's the first time; it has the potential to literally be a one-off. The second time, it's a warning that it may actually become a habit, because the third time you do it, it's a pattern. A trigger creates the context for the behavior and you get a reward—not that the reward is necessarily positive. The reward of a reaction, no matter how negative, is still a measurable result.

The first visit from my LDR man was idyllic. Off we went in a hired car, driving to my favorite places, seeing the sights, having lovely food and pints of Guinness. I'd had the idea from somewhere that he didn't drink, so I was surprised when he joined me. But he brushed off my query, saying that he was able "to pat the beast," so I forgot about it and returned to enjoying every moment.

We found we had a similar fondness for stretches of under-populated majestic coastline, such as Loop Head in County Clare. We both liked just getting in the car and driving, perhaps coming across something unexpected, like the time we were chasing down a holy well and almost got bogged down in a field when the road inexplicably disappeared. We could both appreciate the weight of history found on the sites of medieval monasteries, the like of Clonmacnoise in County Offaly. That he was there, seeing all the things I had fallen in love with, made me feel like I could fall in love with him, too.

Back and forth we went: He came back to Ireland to help me make a short film, I flew over to New York to work briefly for my former employer. After almost a year of Long Distance Relating, somehow we came to the decision that he would move abroad—"somehow" because I don't remember either of us consciously making that choice. I suppose there had been talk of the future, and if I would return to the United States, to which I said no. There was a job he claimed he'd been trying to leave for years, and I had excellent connections in Dublin that we thought would open doors…it would be exciting…we'd figure it out as we went along.

Except I was doing most of the figuring. I didn't go so far as to book his flight (this time) but I found him a storage place in New York "he might want to look into," gathered links to job sites and networked with acquaintances to find out who might be looking for help. Sometimes I'd call or email, and he wouldn't respond for a day or two…and to battle my fear that he was changing his mind, that I would lose him, I worked harder to ensure that everything would be perfect when he arrived. A little voice peeped occasionally in my ear, asking if I was going a bit overboard, if I was doing too much. But no, I told myself, he was making the sacrifice of leaving home, so the least I could do was arrange everything on my end.

There was a worrying silence the week before his big arrival. I didn't mention my concern to any of my friends, because what if, after all this buildup, he backed out? What then?

We managed little more than a cursory chat the night before he left. I didn't sleep well, but made my way to the airport to meet his early morning flight, leaving the shared house I was living in hours and hours before the plane was to land. A slowly increasing crowd waited for loved ones, the acoustics in the terminal making every announcement over the hubbub reverberate as if it was coming from on high. I kept getting up to use the bathroom, and changing my seat to see which would have the best view of the arrivals door. The monitor displayed the news his plane had touched down, had reached the gate.

Excited greetings rose around me as embraces were exchanged by those reunited, the noise level building and building until it was deafening; the dearth of sleep plus the anticipation and trepidation plus the shrieking and whooping equaled sensory overload. My breathing was shallow and my head was spinning and I just wanted him to *get there* so we could leave. When he arrived, I'd have an anchor in all this noise and madness. When he arrived, I might give out a shriek or whoop myself. When he arrived, I'd feel settled, centered.

When he came through customs, looking rough, angry, and not especially happy to be there, I found myself thinking: *What have I done?*

It was the kind of morning that caused Dubliners to remark to one another, known and unknown, "What a day!" Bright, clear, blue sky, the sun with some heat in it but that nip in the air. Simply gorgeous. I was as excited to get to my lesson that day as I was my very first time—as excited as if I was still that early in the journey, a realization that only enhanced my sense of pure joy.

I was stuffed full to the brim with well-being.

Until Roisin told me to take Dancer.

I drooped like a petulant child. "Can't I have Maverick?" I whined—I did, I absolutely did, I whined—and Roisin, who is patience on a monument, as they say, showed me the list with all of his hours on it, and I slouched off to the barn.

I stomped down the aisle, sighing heavily as I grabbed Dancer's gear and tacked him up. "Listen, dude," I said, trying to be authoritative and yet...friendly? This was already, I guessed, not such a great approach. "Let's just...*go* today, okay?" I sounded less convincing than beseeching. Nope, not good.

I led Dancer into the arena; some of the new parents gaped as we walked by, because he was, in fact, enormous, and frankly, that puffed me up. Oh, sure, I can handle this guy! I walked him up to a patch of light, because the last time I rode him, he seemed to be really spooky around little "puddles" of sun. He was keen, however, on unearthing something edible from the ground. Roisin said we were going to the outside ring, and I perked up; hell, it was nothing but sunshine out there today. It might be okay.

It wasn't okay. Dancer still wouldn't go when I asked him to go. Or he would go for a bit, lulling me into a false sense of security, and then stop dead. We made it through circles and serpentines and then started jumping, which was going great guns until the last one, one last time through a little series of two fences. I got him going, after a concerted effort involving legs and taps on his bum, and while he was cutting the approach to the first obstacle kind of short, at least he was moving. Then four strides out from the first fence he broke into a canter, and I was mentally thrown off, although we got over clear.

And I then I did it *again*: I started to jump the second fence before Dancer did, and there was this feeling of the world (Dancer) crashing to a halt as I kept going.

My sixth fall.

I raised myself halfway to my knees, and Roisin was there beside me, wearing a concerned look, albeit one lacking in surprise. Dancer hadn't moved.

"Can I go again." It was a statement rather than a question.

"Of course," Roisin replied, and she went to get a mounting block.

Dancer looked at me—contrite? I clambered to my feet beside him. He dipped his head and rubbed my nose inquisitively with his own. We looked each other obliquely in the eye, and stood, neck to neck, until Roisin returned.

I climbed back into the saddle. Dancer and I took the two fences at the trot, cleanly.

On the bus ride home, I thought to myself, One more to go...

Once I began to ride horses, I no longer had conventional weekends. I didn't go out for pints on Friday because I was riding Saturday, and I didn't go out to dinner on Saturday because I had spent all my money on lessons that morning. Sundays were spent doing the beginning of the week's work so I could take a private lesson Monday. I went grudgingly on vacation but made sure it was either a horseback-riding holiday or figured out a way to get an hour's lesson in wherever I was. (Once I'd been riding for a dozen years, I didn't feel quite so terrified that I was going to forget everything I'd learned if I took a few weeks off. I began to see the benefit of taking a break.)

But honestly, I don't really care about going anywhere, anymore. I have been thoroughly domesticated.

As long as I can remember, I have always wanted to be someplace else. My Irish grandmother lived in Astoria, and occasionally, on the way home from a visit, my father would drive through Manhattan. I was eight, cuddled up in the back of the station wagon, in the seat that faced the oncoming traffic. When I looked up and saw the Empire State Building, lit up like Christmas, I knew I wanted to live in the city.

Dublin wasn't New York. I did not love it. Not at first. When I moved to Ireland in 1998, it was during the unheard era of national prosperity that became known as the Celtic Tiger (an unrealistic economy that was a result of direct investment from foreign corporations and a property price bubble). But despite the newfound vitality and prosperity, nothing worked. It took forever to get a latté to go, and that was after it took me three days to find a place that did takeaway coffee at all. I ranted (unreasonably) at a friend when the computer keyboard I'd ordered was going to take two weeks to arrive. *Two weeks!* I'd gone from living in a place where you received goods almost before you thought of buying them, to some ridiculous backwater where it would take fourteen days to obtain standard office equipment. Fact was, I hadn't moved to Ireland so I could live in a city that didn't have skinny venti mochas and instant gratification. My trips had focused on the countryside, and everything you read about it is true. It is absolutely spectacular. It is as green as it is said to be, the people are extraordinarily friendly, so willing to take you as you are, and the views along the western coastline are humbling and profound.

But Dublin...Dublin is a rabbit warren of twisty streets and nondescript facades, with people who look right through you and are shockingly gruff and unhelpful.

Until you have proven that you are *there*. "There" as in "there to stay," as well as "right there with them." It takes learning the lingo, learning how to be the absolute correct degree of brusque, which is offhand enough to let the other know that you know what's what but not so ungracious that you won't take time to have a chat, or a moan, or a laugh. Once you have proven that you aren't just passing through, that you aren't on your way to a museum or the zoo, you get a pass, and even if taxi drivers persist in querying your country of origin twenty years later, you fit in. You find a handful of alleyways and back streets that make you feel like a local and get you around town in no time, and you still get a buzz off living in a foreign country, off having developed a career and made friends, and there's a thrill to it still, but somehow, with an element of balance, too, of roots sunk, of the unfamiliar made dearly familiar and yet with discoveries still to be made.

This sense of wonder is something I recovered. As challenging as I found settling down in a foreign country, my partner had it worse. There was no honeymoon period—we may have used it up, over the long distance. My connections regarding his work panned out, but there was always something wrong with the job; I fully supported his desire to pursue his dream of being an artist, but the teachers weren't good enough, or the life-drawing studio was crowded and poorly lit, or the school was too far from home. I found an academy in our neighborhood; he didn't apply in time. I suggested other job openings; he didn't like the situation, or the pay, or his colleagues. Every time an obstacle appeared I flung myself over it, through it, underneath it, full of ideas, certain of success.

What I assumed in the first few weeks was jet lag...wasn't. His mood was forbidding, and despite my excitement, which was beginning to feel strained, there was a palpable lack of joy and optimism and life, all the hallmarks of the early days of a developing relationship. He spent the first weeks hunkered down in the house and every now and again exploring the city. When he came back from a potential gig, he had nothing but disdain for the way the company did things.

One night I came home from work to a lovely dinner and a very drunk dude. He'd never over-imbibed in the year we'd been an LDR, or at least not that I knew. I was shocked as the laughing and dancing and carrying on devolved into knocking into furniture and breaking things as a consequence; he glowered at me when I suggested we put the wine away, and then descended into a sulky silence.

It wasn't what I wanted to live with, at all.

The next morning, I carefully brought it up, explaining
that I wasn't comfortable with what went on, that I had thought
his drinking wasn't an issue?

Shrug. He was sorry.

Was he struggling with the move?

Maybe. He guessed so.

I took a deep breath. Did he suffer from depression?
Because it seemed like he was pretty down, most of the time—

No, he didn't.

Okay. Would therapy help him acclimate? I sure had
needed it!

Didn't need it.

What followed was the first rendition of The Speech, the
first round of imploring and promising. He said he'd stop drinking. And he mostly did.

We went back to normal, the early days of discovery and
fun, and the life I'd dreamed of began—until the next wave
of misery and discord surged out of nowhere. I couldn't make
excuses for him, couldn't blame the time change anymore. The
pattern of dysfunction was starting to take shape.

We were out in one of Kilternan's fields so we could practice over
the "natural" cross-country fences, three in a row. Delilah loved
being outside, away from the walls and fences that defined the
rings, and she was unusually forward-going. The mini-course
went slightly uphill over some tires, then a plank fence, then up
and around to a log, maybe a foot and a half, not high.

As we came around, Delilah felt...sluggish? I struggled, as
usual, to get her straight, approaching the log, knowing she'd pop
over the fence sideways if she could, and then we were airborne...

Her landing was wrong, something was off—did she stumble? I felt myself going head over heels to the right, and I landed with a bang, and I couldn't—I couldn't breathe. I thought I was probably fine, nothing was likely broken; I was okay, except for the part where I felt like I was going to suffocate.

I gasped and hollered. I was pretty sure I'd never hollered in my life, but it was an animalistic reaction to not being able to breathe. I was conscious that air was not entering my lungs as it should, and I panted in distress.

"Got the wind knocked out of you?" Niamh called out as she trotted over to help.

"Yeah," I wheezed, finally restored to the autonomic function I swore I would never take for granted again. I sat up. I breathed and breathed some more. Delilah fucked off down the field, no sympathy for me this time. This time it was my fault.

Once I retrieved her and got back on, our group proceeded to one of the upper fields to canter, and for the first time in a long time, I wasn't sure I knew how to stay on, how to stay balanced, how to *do* this.

Why was I doing this, again?

No! I thought. I am not giving this up!

We cantered up the field.

We walked back down to the indoor arena.

My seventh fall. So I was now a *rider*. But my fear of the great outdoors was back.

"All right?" asked Roisin.

"Bit sore," I replied.

Did I think that seven falls were going to be it? Did I think some miraculous transformation was going to take place after a handful of times hitting the dirt? Yeah. I did. I thought that having survived the necessary seven falls, I'd be elevated into a higher realm of competence and skill. I almost believed that I'd never fall again.

I was so wrong. The night before my private lesson with Roisin, I was on Maverick and facing a triple jump combination. A triple in the indoor arena was pretty tight. I got nervous. He picked up on this, and as was his wont, took advantage of it. We went pelting at the fences and upon landing, I was off balance... so off balance I was desperately clinging to the saddle with my right knee. Mav kindly dropped his inside shoulder (brat!) and swung his bum around so I was flung up against the wall. I scraped my elbow (the first bloodletting) then slammed to the ground, and lost my wind again.

But when Roisin asked how I was, less than twenty-four hours later, I didn't tell her how much I was aching. I couldn't believe that I was there, to be honest. But that horsemanlike stoicism appealed to me—so, I was only "a bit sore"—and besides, I knew no one was going to mollycoddle me, anyway. Every horseperson knows how much learning to ride hurts, and that, despite the hurting, you have to carry on, because if you don't carry on, you will quit, and if you quit, you will never be the same, because once the horses get in there—get in your heart—you're screwed if you can't be around them.

It's exactly the same when someone—a person—has gotten into your heart, and you see him doing things that are counter-intuitive, making choices that result in frustration for him and discomfort and guilt for yourself. You love this person, and you don't want to give up on him, give up on the two of you as a couple, give up on the idea that this is the man you want to marry.

After Fall Seven, somebody else told me that it actually takes *one hundred* falls to make a rider. I'm certainly well over halfway there, although now I don't need some artificial bench-mark to validate whether or not I am a "rider." I know that the only way to become a rider is to ride. If you can't get up and go again after the falls, then you won't ride, and therefore, you will not become a rider.

If there's one thing I have learned as I've gained my hundred falls, it's that when I don't speak up, I always end up on my ass.

I took a spectacularly bad tumble off Ruby, in which a short stretch of unconsciousness ensued, and all because I didn't say, before retaking a jump combination in the indoor arena, "Um, she feels a bit crazy to me." Upon landing after the second fence the mare took off at great speed, heading straight for the doors of the arena, and then I opened my eyes to find myself on the ground. It was twenty minutes before I remembered the lesson and what happened. I went to the hospital, just in case.

I never jumped Ruby again.

Despite the warning bells I heard, despite sensing Ruby "wasn't right," I couldn't say no in the arena anymore than I had been able say no in other areas of my life. All those times that I said yes, when no was the better response, I have lived to regret. Many times through the course of my marriage, I kept pushing myself to go the distance, even though it was a damned bumpy ride. I wanted love and I wanted approval and I couldn't say no. I had made a commitment, and we would stay the course because I was sure we had more in our favor than the occasionally spaced-out weirdness, the cold silences, the bubbling rage, the drastic shifts in mood. Once it all settled down, it would be fine, once he found a job he enjoyed—then we could get on with the business of the rest of our lives. *It would be fine.*

But there was a stronger something deep inside me that was merely waiting for all the dust to die down, for that last fall to be the worst, for me to lie still enough to take stock and start making some mature decisions. I could see the reality of the situation; I was somewhat conscious that the made-up world I was constructing was not accurate. I had only to, as they say in twelve-step programs, get off the merry-go-round of denial and get back to reality.

Reality said: if you keep covering all the expenses, it's actually going to be damaging to you and to him.

Reality suggested: you need to get your own particular brand of crazy under control.

Reality warned: this situation could become unsafe for you in a heartbeat. All it would take was the wrong word, the wrong request, and all that rage would explode.

Reality made sense. I could absolutely agree with Reality. I knew I had to get out.

Why did it seem so damn hard, though?

What was I so afraid of?

CHAPTER FOUR

FEAR

I woke up one Saturday, swamped with fear. "Swamped" because it felt like I was immersed in a cold dampness, seeping into my skin, like I had slept the night in a puddle of dank, icy water. I was shivering.

And I knew what had made me awaken in this state: I was afraid to go to my lesson and ride Maverick.

I had only recently begun to ride him again following an ornate injury I had gotten, riding a different horse. The healing was ongoing, and would be for some time, but I was whole enough to get back in the saddle—and on Maverick in particular. It had been a bad week, two weeks previous: I had fallen off him twice in two lessons. *Twice* in two lessons! For some reason, this had only just sunk in.

I had fear oozing from my pores. I was afraid to ride him, pure and simple. And I didn't know what I was going to do.

I was no stranger to this feeling.

One morning, months after I had left my marriage for good, I woke up, panicking. In that moment I understood what it meant to have one's "blood run cold." I once thought it was a literary flourish, but now I knew no one made that up out of nothing. Though I was barely awake, my skin shivered with cold sweat, and my throat tensed up as if I wanted to scream but couldn't. My heart was palpitating. I was dreading full consciousness even before I realized I wasn't fully conscious.

In August 2005 I left the marital home and moved into a bedsit, which is an old-fashioned Irish term for what a New Yorker might call a studio apartment. "Studio" sounds far more dashing than this was, however—no, this was the kind of room inhabited by an aged bachelor left alone in the world. The tiny bathroom was up the stairs from the main space, which held a table and a chair, a kitchenette, a clothes cupboard, and a single bed. The main room was blessed with a lofty Georgian ceiling, which eased the pain of the (very) small square footage. It was on the ground floor, and I was fairly certain that the musty carpet was laid right over said ground: it was always cold and damp, and I left the space heater on at all times. (The first electricity bill was breathtaking.)

I was incredibly grateful for this little place. As frightened as I was when I took it—an action born of panic rather than resolution—I was, even then, very aware that the signing of that lease was my first big step forward.

The steps before had been small...but nevertheless, bone-rattlingly difficult. I had learned about detachment from twelve-step meetings: There is nothing worse than asking a codependent to step back, to step away—except, perhaps, asking an alcoholic to refuse a drink. I found my breath was my friend, and if I could just breathe, I could stop the endless chatter in my mind exhorting me to just go back to doing what was familiar (chase, nag, rationalize, fix, fix, fix). I went for a swim at the gym down the road, I reached out to my new friends from my twelve-step program, and I breathed and breathed.

The end of my marriage wasn't pretty. It could have been worse, though—and I say that not as someone who used to make excuses for everything, but as someone who, when the end did come, consciously prayed for grace and dignity.

You see, after some time in the bedsit, and after some work on myself, I decided I was going to end the separation and move into a New Place with my husband. This way, our lives could be different (despite all evidence to the contrary). Ah, the magic of a New Place! Where nothing bad *had* happened, so that nothing bad *would ever* happen. In order to get to the New Place, I would:

1) Deny another binge.
2) Ignore the altercations with police, when he was caught stealing a bicycle.
3) Dismiss incidents in which he claimed to have been jumped by gangs but were in truth fracases he initiated.

Never mind all that: we were going to have a New Place, a new beginning, the keys all ours, the lease signed.

The evening before the day we were to move in, he called me as I was on my way to leave some belongings in the house—one in a recent series of lunatic phone calls, the kind with which I was intimately familiar. They always came in the middle of The Cycle. He was about to lose yet another job.

I got off the bus, went back to my bedsit and...I don't know what happened in my brain between the call and my tiny studio, but I suddenly knew I wasn't going to go there. Literally. I spent that night talking and listening to trusted friends, and in the morning, I canceled the whole thing. No New Place, no marriage, no nothing.

No nothing.

I spent the weekend going to twelve-step meetings, reaching out for help, dodging his phone calls, which became crazy, angry voicemails, and somehow sticking to my decision. But I paid another month's rent on the Old Place, the one we used to live in together, where now only he slept, when he slept. I allowed the landline to remain activated, taking care of the bill. I did these things and did them without qualm because I knew they would be the last things I did as a participant in the dysfunctional, unbalanced situation. I took a van-shaped taxi to our old house, grabbed a random bunch of boxes that I hoped were full of my things, unloaded them in my bedsit, and cried and breathed, breathed and cried.

I thought that was the scariest thing I would ever do in my entire life.

Despite continuing to improve week to week, lesson to lesson, I always suffered a tiny niggle of nerves whenever I got on a horse I hadn't ridden before. Even though I'd seen Maverick ridden by others many times, when I mounted him for the first time, none of that made a difference: he was new to me, I was new to him, and I was fully aware there was bound to be a learning curve.

Maverick would forever be my...nemesis? Archenemy? When he was bad, he was rotten. But then there was the time I jumped over three feet on him—a gloriously unexpected event, during what looked to be a usual lesson. We'd been routinely jumping a few fences around two feet high—I think. It's impossible to gauge height from horseback. Everything looks low, until it gets higher.

Picking up the canter, we took a few fences cleanly. All in a day's work. Niamh shouted, "Come again!" As we cantered a half-circle around to the approach once more, that's when I noticed that the top rail had gone up well over two feet—another six inches? More? I kept Maverick going in the turn toward the fence: his ears were up and my bum was in the saddle, stride-stride-stride-stride-stride, bum out of the saddle, up and over—

"Come again!"

We started to come again, and I looked toward the fence, as I'm meant to in these exercises, and as I came down the long side of the arena, I...I may have squeaked.

"Don't look!" Niamh called with a laugh as Maverick started to cut the corner. I sat on my bum, shortened the reins, straightened him out, looked up, breathed, and stride-stride-stride-stride, then we flew, with power and speed, up and over a fence that was higher than anything I'd ever jumped.

"Yeah!" I shouted as we landed, me imperfectly, a bit heavy on his neck, Mav only slightly jigging to the right. I apologized to the group for shouting. I suppose I felt that I had betrayed any trace of burgeoning equestrian cool with my gleeful bellow.

Then, there was the time we were in the lower arena, and I swear to God, he glanced over his shoulder at me as we passed a big juicy mud puddle as if to say, *Got your name on it, babe.* And sure enough, he landed me in it.

But then there was the time we were doing transitions, and he gave me walk-to-canter—which is really hard to get him to do, much harder than going from the faster pace of trot into canter—and nobody could believe it. But I believed we could do it, and so we did.

I have heard it said, "From the brain to the rein," and it's true even though it sounds nuts: Whatever you are thinking is communicated to the horse, through your hands on the reins, through your legs on his sides, through your bum in the saddle. The slightest twitch can tell the horse more than you yourself are aware of, and once you make a horse nervous, well, it's all over. Example: We were jumping and came around to the fence, and one stride away, Maverick ran out. Dodged it. I had, in my mind, momentarily thought, Crap, that's high, which caused me to pinch my buttocks in trepidation and drop the bit—so, he ran out...because he couldn't trust me to trust him over the obstacle.

How much did I inspire Maverick to misbehave? I'd certainly done my time as an enabler, and I knew that he was only giving back what he got—or so they said in horsey circles. Did I need to start working on what I was giving out? Maybe my boundaries needed to be stronger? Did we need to take a break, maybe, give each other some space? My relationship with Maverick was starting to feel all too familiar.

It must be said that there is a requisite amount of fear required when one mounts a horse. Although I'm actually not sure the correct word is in fact "fear"...nor is it "trepidation," nor "dread"...it is definitely not "panic." It is more like being "properly afraid." "Appropriately cautious?" It is having a conscious awareness that anything could happen, and that all I can do is stay balanced, keep a good contact, behave calmly in challenging circumstances, and make corrections as I go along. This is basically what I should be doing in a relationship with a human:

1) Keep a good ratio of "me" time and "us" time.
2) Communicate clearly and listen well.
3) Be willing to respond in the moment rather than react.
4) Keep an open mind.

As prey animals, horses might be, at best, described as vigilant; at worst, they always seem to expect the shit to hit the fan. The slightest thing sets them right off: the flap of black plastic loosened from a bale of hay; an empty snack packet fluttering along the road; a bird flushed out of a bush. Because they always expect to be terrified, they easily can be, and it is in fact kind of amazing that they're not always going around in a state of hyper-reactivity.

The reason they don't is because, again as prey animals, they are always looking for a leader, and we two-legged types, since we also supply food and shelter, have assumed the role. When someone else is in charge, all is well, and horses can mostly ignore the flapping plastic, the crazy birds, and go about their work with a minimum of fuss.

However...when the supposed leader exhibits anything that resembles the kind of fear the horse feels at any given time, then the works are officially bespannered, and all hell is at its highest potential to break loose. Here's a cool fact: Have you ever noticed that when you're afraid, you hold your breath? If you're up on top of a horse, this is a really bad thing to do. I've read that their hereditary memory of being preyed upon has loads to do with predators leaping at them from above—the mountain lion, say, would quickly intake its breath as it pounced. So there you are, determined to give this horseback riding lark a go, forget to breathe, and the animal beneath you decides you must be about to eat him.

And it all devolves from there.

Horses give out only that which they receive because, as prey, they are prepared to react to changes in their surroundings. They have evolved as a species due to this alertness and preparedness. "Horses have ensured their...survival through highly sensitive observational skills and intuitive responses," writes Equine Experiential Learning facilitator Wendy Golding, for the online magazine *Equine Leadership*. "Unlike humans who rely mainly in their intellect, horses access the wisdom of their entire bodies, allowing them to read and respond to all the energies around them." The energies of the rider are a significant aspect of the horse's environment; even non-horsey people are aware that a horse can pick up on their nerves. If you're calm and controlled, they will be as well; if you're shaking in your boots...well, things can get messy.

Fear. It can be about so many things, in humans and horses. It can be general distress when one's world order is mucked up. It can be specific, like a phobia. It can galvanize, enabling a mother to lift the car under which her child is trapped. It can paralyze, as a reaction to extreme physical trauma. It can be bad for you, causing you to hold on when you should really let go...or it can actually be good for you, like the fear that takes hold before you sit for an exam, which sharpens your focus and allows everything else that is nonessential to stay out of the way.

Biologically, fear is a response that unleashes chemicals that are not nearly as nice as those that surge through the system when you fall in love. With fear, you get epinephrine, not endorphins, and the parts of the brain that engage are different: The thalamus and sensory cortex react and interpret data, respectively, your hippocampus picks out a context—Car crash? Did I study sufficiently?—then your amygdala runs through its stored memories of frightening events to further hone the response of your hypothalamus, which decides on fight or flight or freeze.

That's the so-called "High Road." When fear takes the High Road, you've got time to think, even if it's only one or two moments of assessment. When fear takes the "Low Road," you go from the thalamus, race through the amygdala, and flail into the hypothalamus. The body reacts by making lots of stress-based hormones, which can result in heart palpitations, or a cold sweat, or an inability to focus on the big picture.

The general horseback-riding-related situations that can result in fear are diverse in their outcomes, but the essential feeling doesn't enjoy much variation: you are up there, something happens, the horse reacts, and then you react (or not). Perhaps that's why it takes seven (or a hundred) falls to make a rider. A rider has the worst-case scenaria filed away because she's lived them: *all* the falls—from the time she gently flumped to the ground in what felt like slow motion, to the time she was thrown into the door and knocked unconscious, to the time she fell off twice when trying to mount (the second fall being the one in which she slid down her horse's off side and squeaked, "Help!" as he went skipping for the arena door).

So if Maverick jigged to the side in a spook, it wasn't really that big a deal. My hippocampus went, *Feh,* and I'd sit back and ride it out. *My* body recognized how *his* body bunched up when he was going to jump sideways and cut off the panic. My old "Monday horse," Joxer, was a big dude, and I'd never fallen off him. One winter afternoon, I made it up the slippery road to my lesson, picking my way carefully over the ice, and figured if anything bad was ever going to happen with Joxer, it was going to be that day. I noticed the farm tractor revving up outside the arena, and as I swung into the saddle, I knew I didn't want Joxer to realize that I was rather *too* aware of it, so I concentrated on keeping my composure. Of course, just as I was thinking we were in the clear, the little smokestack—or whatever it is on the top of those machines—let out a teeny puff of smoke and sound. I thought, uh oh, felt Joxer bunch, and then I again sat back, even laughed, as he lunged away from the terrifying, unknown emission.

Then there are the times when a thing happens, and you don't really know it's happening, and then it's happening, and time as you know it foreshortens, and your hippocampus doesn't seem too worried, although the thalamus is going, *Hmmm.* In one of my first group lessons on Cathal, that sturdy cob, we were cantering all together—eight riders, eight horses—and the four-leggeds were gettin' excited. Playtime! Race! There we were, coming around to the A end of the arena, and then all of a sudden, as I passed F, I was thinking: This is kinda fast.

At B, I thought: Yeah, this is—whoops.

As we were just about to pass M, I wondered: Am I going to fall off? Maybe I should bail?

As we passed C, I finally mumbled: "Uh—whoa!"

Imagine my relief when Cathal stopped on a dime behind the rider in front of us.

That was four thoughts in six seconds—actually five, as I managed two at M. (I think for one second, between F and B, I sat back and enjoyed myself.) It was so fast, I didn't even know how I was thinking or reacting. I wasn't afraid until M, and then I figured out that we had to stop eventually. Or Cathal did. Or something. Something happened that prevented a bad outcome, and I like to think it was because I didn't panic.

"From the brain to the rein." Just before some of my falls, I *knew* I was going to come off. If I have that fear in my body, then it's surely being communicated to my mount.

With riding, it's as much in my head as it is in my hands and my seat. If I can stop a horse just with my bum—and the well-trained ones respond to a twitch of ass-muscles like you wouldn't believe—then can I cause my own problems with my thoughts?

Hmmm.

When I woke up frightened, that post-marriage morning, I woke on the Low Road. And the thing was, I wasn't even afraid for myself, I was afraid for my ex, and terrified I'd been wrong when I had confronted him about how I knew he was misusing pharmaceuticals again, just before we were about to move into the New Place. He denied he was using; I knew he was lying: we'd had another one of those meals where he was swaying over his plate, nearly falling off the chair. And yet, months later, despite every sign I'd learn to recognize over the course of our years together, I woke up thinking I'd been mistaken. Maybe he'd only been tired/had been feeling unwell/was preoccupied about losing the latest job. I thought I'd fucked it up, broken the marriage all by myself because (maybe?) I had misinterpreted his mood.

I woke up mid-panic. What was he doing? Was he all right? Where was he living? Had he gotten all his stuff out of Ireland and back to the States? Had I made a huge mistake? How was he going to cope? I was in a codependent sweat, and God help me, it took me the rest of the day to get the breath back in my body.

In contrast, the fear I felt on the bus, riding to my first lesson, was unarticulated. I tried to turn it into another thing, like the flu I "felt coming on," but when it came down to it, I was afraid of the unknown. Or rather, I feared the *known* thing, of falling off and hurting myself, as I had on that first ill-conceived trail ride. The thing was, though, that I had said I was going to do this thing, this ride-on-a-horse thing, and I was a champion when it came to doing what I said I was going to do.

There's integrity, and then there's stubbornness.

Stubbornness was the defining characteristic of my relationship with Maverick. In the beginning, I was actually flattered that I was assigned him to ride. When I had seen him in other lessons, I considered those piloting him 'round to be the good riders. And the first few times I had him, it went really well. Like, really, really well. It was amazing, and I looked forward to my lessons with a new vigor and excitement. It was like that new crush: Ooh, he's cute and seems smart and is good at what he does—I like him! Everything went so well those first weeks riding Mav, I started to think I had found "my" horse, the right horse for me.

Ah, the honeymoon period. I learned that this was how Maverick lulled a rider into a false sense of security. This was where he assessed all the things that the rider couldn't do, and then proceeded, one by one, to exploit every weakness.

Bad balance? Well, then, upon landing after a jump, let me drop my shoulder just as you are almost back in the saddle, and I'll veer off sharply to the left or right, whichever, I'm not fussy, and see if you stay on. Insecure in your aids? Unassertive? Hmm, let's see, how's about I never, ever give you the canter depart? I'll just sloooooow down to a walk, and then when you kick, or tap me up with the stick, I'll buck and buck. Want me to stop once you do get the canter going? You better mean it, sister. All the things that were "wrong" with him painfully highlighted all the things that were "wrong" with me.

But why, oh, why, did I stick with him?

I didn't beat myself up by asking, why ride a horse at all? I'd already explained *that* insanity to myself. But why did I hesitate when my hippocampus presented me with enough context to make a healthy decision? Why didn't I listen when my thalamus was quite sensibly telling me what to do?

Stubborn. Stubborn as muck. Didn't want to be seen as a quitter. Didn't want to fail in public. Wanted to come across as resilient, unfazed. I toughed it out because I was afraid to feel foreboding and anxiety. I was afraid that if I admitted that I was afraid at a single, precise moment, then I was going to be afraid for all the moments that were ever going to come for the rest of my life.

Feelings were always scary to me: I never had feelings, they always had me. I didn't know how to express them in the present moment, so I held on to them until they built and built, and then I exploded.

I began to experiment with telling the truth about what I was feeling. It was a slow, halting process, and it came upon me unexpectedly; the more I rode, the less I could lie about what was going on inside myself. If I didn't want to hold fear in my body, I had to get it out somehow, and talking to other horse people seemed a good place to start. I found myself telling others at the barn about my falls. I started with the kids, because I thought they were more likely to understand. Kids are allowed to fall. Kids are still permitted to be afraid.

In return for my war stories, I was told harrowing tales of tumbles and crashes. I was shown scars. We all agreed that the only thing to do was "get back up there." I got something else from the young ones: the absence of lingering fear, the total belief that the next time it wouldn't be so bad, that any experience was what you made of it, that even the ones that didn't work out the way you wanted were still worthwhile, because you were always learning, and it was always worth trying something new.

A friend texted me to meet up for a drink, and I replied that I couldn't as I was going to the barn after work to jump a course. A full one. With many fences in a row. And spectators. And ribbons for the winners. It was like a mini-show, a "clear-round" competition, whatever that meant.

Was I? Really? I had my eye on the sky all day, waiting for the predicted deluge, hoping for it. I called the barn to see if the jumping was still on, and provoked distress in the woman who answered the phone. She asked, "Why wouldn't it be on?" and then we both got anxious about the weather. The thing was,

I was going to go all the way out there, and the jumping was to be in the upper outdoor arena, and if it rained, I'd have gone all the way out there for nothing, when I could have been sinking a few pints and *not* been jumping, jumping a course I'd never seen before, in a competitive scenario.

As soon as I got on the bus, it started to rain. I tried to reckon the direction of the scattering shower, and it looked like it was blowing out to sea. My earphones were too loud for me to realize that my phone was ringing, and I missed the call...but the message left said the show was still on.

I got to the barn. I walked up to the office, paid my fee, requested Delilah, put on my helmet and reckoned that I better take a look at the course.

I stood outside the gate for moment, trying to work out the round from a distance. Then I noticed another lady walking around the fences, gauging the approaches. I went in and joined her. She talked me through the course, and it all started to make sense.

"I've never done this before," I admitted. "I'm nervous."

"You'll be fine once you get out there." She smiled, and I smiled, and I went to get Delilah.

I tacked the mare up, only realizing at that very moment that there was no one around to hold her while I mounted. I had tried, once before, to mount her without a restraining hand...and it hadn't worked. Well, I had to get on her to jump this course, so get on her I would. I led Delilah to the indoor arena, talking her through it as she grumpily chewed on a handful of hay that she'd snaffled from the ground. I'm getting up on this horse, I told myself, and grabbing a healthy amount of rein, I put my foot in the stirrup and swung up.

As we walked toward the upper arena, I thought, I have done this all by myself! I'd tacked her, mounted her, and was now walking her up to the jumping ring, all by myself, like a proper rider, like a person who rides horses.

Things were looking up.

Someone opened the gate for me and I immediately took stock. I had no idea what to do, what the etiquette was. I knew we needed to warm up, to have a few goes at the practice fence—which sat well away from the course, and over which people were already schooling their mounts—but otherwise, I didn't have a clue. A few riders were trotting their horses in the general flow of the fences, so I did it, too.

Okay: Fence Number One was at C, Number Two was at X, Three at A, then a combination (two fences with only a few strides between them), counted as Number Four at E, then back to the first fence, which was now Five. Six and Seven were set along the B side of the arena, and Eight was roughly at X again.

Right.

Delilah and I trotted, we cantered, we popped over the practice fence a few times, which was fairly hairy as people kept changing direction. Delilah grudgingly took the small cross-rail, and we knocked it down once in the canter before trying the fence again after the poles had been reset.

Okay. Okay. (Crap.)

Then the first rider set off over the course, kindly wishing us all luck, and suddenly I was ready to go. Suddenly, it wasn't that big a deal. There we were: up in the upper arena, jumping a course. There we were, cantering around, taking the first fence, getting a good line into the second, then the third, a bit of hesitation on Delilah's part with the second fence in the combination, and then...

...and then I just blanked. If you'd asked me my name, I would probably have just shaken my head in confusion. I saw the next fence. I saw the figure "5" on the placard on one side. Delilah kept cantering. I kept looking at the number "5," and as we winged by it, I reckoned I'd better circle back and jump the thing rather than just keep going...and then on to Numbers Six, Seven, Eight, taken, nothing falling down (including me), and before I knew it, I'd done it.

"First clear round!" shouted a boy who was waiting his turn.

Really? No, that couldn't be right. That was a fault at Number Five, wasn't it? For one shining moment, I thought I had it, that first-place ribbon, in my hot little hand. Everyone in the warm-up area congratulated me; no one had seen me drift in the middle of the course—except for the guy managing the competition so, no, it wasn't a clear round, but...I did it!

I was immersed in a world I'd never imagined being part of, in a reality where everybody sat on their horses and talked to me, and I talked to them, and I received compliments and gave them, and I felt like, if my feet weren't in the stirrups, I would have just floated away on a cloud of joy and achievement and sheer awesomeness.

I beamed the entire way home, watching all the dressed up people heading out to restaurants and bars, delighted with myself, and my damp head, and my mucky boots.

But, oh, how I wanted that ribbon...

There is a requisite amount of fear required when one enters into a marriage. I don't think the word, in this case, needs to be qualified. You know you're availing of an institution that attracts statistical criticism like manure attracts flies, and yet you think that, despite everything, you can make a go of it. That's human nature, maybe, and oxytocin, certainly. You choose to take the leap knowing that a horde of researchers is waving reams of paper at you, shouting percentages, yet you plow on, regardless. There is a degree of self-deception here that is societally acceptable, perhaps even required.

The thing is, no one tells you the truth about marriage. Or if they do, it is already too late. That first year, even if you've known each other forever or been living together or whatever, is just odd. Not because of what might be going on in your relationship (and in my case there was already plenty), but because it can feel as though you have been abandoned by society. Like everyone you know is thinking, "You are now legal and binding, so no need to keep an eye on you anymore!" Few of our Irish friends were married, and I found it hard to rely on those we knew back in the States. (It's an awkward kind of phone conversation, the kind where you ask if marriage, the actual physical thing of wedding one to the other in front of witnesses, makes everything really, really hard? Harder than it was before?)

Is the mindset "'til death do us part" so inexorable that it serves to destroy a relationship altogether?

Not that I would have expected useful answers, even had there been someone to ask. I figured others lied about their relationships because I was always lying about mine. I'd watch couples, out and about, and wonder what their lives were *really* like. Those two kissing on the corner—had they just spent the last five days ignoring each other and were just now "back to normal?" That pair waiting for the bus, close, but not touching—were they silent out of accord or discord? Was there just the right amount of space between them or too much? And those two over there, laughing and smiling and looking gorgeous: Does he smack her around? Does she hit back? I was living a life that looked like one thing on the outside, but was something entirely different on the inside, and I thought maybe other people had it the same.

On the outside, my marriage looked the way I wanted things to look: attractive man on my arm, personable, funny. Both of us were arty and involved in work that was creative, with a variety of pursuits and passions that made us interesting. And we had time to be together, as we were both self-employed. We could do the shopping together, or take a lovely long walk into town to get a couple of DVDs, a big order of Indian takeout and spend the day in bed, watching the sort of art-house films that we loved, subtitles mandatory, black-and-white a giddy bonus. We'd give dinner parties, he'd cook, and I'd talk, and there would be a turf fire burning in the hearth, and there was smugness and satisfaction in entertaining well, as a couple. We'd have the best times together traveling, sitting in train stations and airports; I would pick the exactly right hotel every time off the Internet, and we'd buy something beautiful to remind us of Prague, or Florence, or Paris. We'd spend evenings reading by the fire, and sometimes I would look up and think, Hey, maybe this could really work.

And yet, I lived in fear.

I lived in fear that I would find myself living with out-of-control, unbridled addiction. I was afraid that it would be incontrovertible, that maybe I was in fact married to a chronic substance misuser. I wiggled around with the truth, to the degree that even though it was clear there was an issue, it was an issue that could be fixed; it was not dependence, which could never be fixed. I made up all sorts of terms and conditions to suit myself, and to suit the story I wanted to tell. There was the one in which I told myself that things weren't actually that bad, because my husband wasn't down-and-out, living on the streets. He was, in fact, able to meet his responsibilities. But in my case, he wasn't living on the streets because I wouldn't let anything go into arrears. He was responsible only for making the dinners.

I could live with that. What I couldn't live with was letting him hit rock bottom; that was too scary for me to imagine.

How was I supposed to sit around and watch that descent? How was I supposed to not pay the whole rent? Such a betrayal seemed impossible. All the recovery books I read said not to enable. They said I should simply do nothing. Others in my twelve-step meetings talked about how they did nothing. But I couldn't do nothing—not in a million years.

If he was going to hit rock bottom, how was I going to avoid hitting it, too?

I don't remember what discrete event triggered the fear, but one day I wasn't afraid, and the next, I was. One day I was happily infatuated with a handsome man who fancied me, and the next, I was worried that he didn't really want to be with me, while at the same time terrified that he *did* want to be with me. I fretted about how largely mood-altering substances figured into the equation of me plus him. I was afraid that this was my last chance to be married and maybe have that baby I might want to have. I was chilled to the bone when I found I could parse his demeanor, his clothing choices, the weight of his tread on the stair, and know how things stood.

The degree of trepidation I experienced on a daily basis, which in turn determined my feelings of security (or not) and optimism (or not), depended on whether doors were slammed or shut gently, whether there was a greeting when he came home, or a response to my own hello when I returned from a day out. I had to know what he was feeling, because then I would know what I was going to feel—or rather, what I was *allowed* to feel. It was nuts, but I assumed a degree of high alert in a very short span of time; almost overnight, I became hypervigilant. I watched, helpless, as the man I loved turned into this other thing, this uncaring, nasty, falling-down-on-the-landing stranger.

Helpless, because anything I offered in the way of succor was rejected, and even though I was aces at managing, all efforts to do so were summarily ignored.

In the first two-thirds of The Cycle, whenever I left the house, I'd experience a feeling of freedom with every step I took through the lovely community in which we lived, greeting the myriad cats that roamed the place like it was a domesticated veldt. Every round of crazy became more and more oppressive. I learned over time to stop talking when we both were home. Silence reigned and the simplest domestic queries were met with refusals: no, he wasn't going to come shopping; no, he didn't care what he ate; no, why would he want me to put some of his things in the laundry? As I passed through the manicured grounds of our neighborhood, peace washed over me. I didn't have to tiptoe around, fend off his anger, swallow my own growing rage. I would go to some freelance gig or other, or interview someone for a magazine article, maybe review a lunchtime play, or meet friends for coffee and a chat, and the weight of the world would lift off my heart. All I had to do was my work, I had the day to myself and my own activities, and I could forget about him...for a few hours.

As I'd head home, though, I'd feel the despair descend, breath by breath. Occasionally a voice in my head demanded, Is this good enough? Is this what you deserve? But by the time I put the key in the door, it was silenced, and I was braced for whatever I was going to find. God forbid that voice found its way out of my mouth—all that ever really amounted to was me dumping shit all over the kitchen table, which only served as unequivocal confirmation to him that I was crazy.

At some stage, I realized that I was Talking, but I wasn't Communicating. This personal insight was akin to throwing down my crutch and walking. Something shifted, something toward a cure, but I didn't have a clue what the hell it meant.

So off I went to the bookstore, a petitioner going to her personal Lourdes, and bought myself a stack of tomes on how to communicate, how not to communicate, what to do if you suspect your partner suffers from depression, what to do to save your marriage, what to do when you have tried to save it and it didn't work, how to say what you meant in a discussion, how to say what you meant in ten seconds or less. I did all the exercises, made notes, journaled, and when I was ready, presented my new, improved style to my partner, who sat there in silence, the occasional shrug his only reaction. A book I read said he was "stonewalling." It was a good term for the insurmountable silence, and its description rang true: a form of confrontation avoidance via a refusal to communicate. It has been described by psychologist Jeffrey Pipe as the "emotional equivalent to cutting off someone's oxygen."

Books can only take one so far, and communicating all by yourself is an utterly useless endeavor. Also, I felt that at least on some level, I was already communicating fine, thanks. I had been communicating ideas as a designer and a writer, and successfully, to boot, for years and years. But the books told me that I wasn't communicating my feelings in a responsible way. I would sulk, and I would cry, but I would never express my anger—at least not in front of him. I would break things, like the door on one of the cabinets in the kitchen, which in a maelstrom of inexpressible frustration got slammed and slammed until the frame cracked.

I was utterly ashamed. And I compounded that shame by pretending, when asked, I didn't have any idea how the cabinet came to be broken.

○

Niamh mounted and said she would take us out to the fields. It had been two or three weeks since my fall at the log.

"Delilah," I whispered. She and I were waiting for me to find a mounting block. "We're going outside the arena. I'm nervous. Easy does it, yeah?"

The mare looked at me. I had learned not to bug her, and how to hold her correctly when I was on the ground so she wouldn't whip her head around and bite me on the belly, and we'd worked out quite a few other things between us. She blinked, nudged me a bit. It seemed she was telling me she understood. I took a breath. Okay.

We went down the lane, then down the road, and we trotted back up. This was fine. I practiced moving gently from my seat when we walked, meaning I was encouraging her to move briskly without flapping around in the saddle. When we trotted it felt nice and light; I wasn't descending too hard on her back. This was okay, too.

We turned into what we called The Three Jump Field, and I breathed. And breathed some more. "Delilah," I whispered again. "Easy, remember?" She was fine, stepping delicately as was her wont, and the group headed for the first obstacle.

"All right?" asked Maureen. She had been there, those weeks ago, at the infamous log.

"Uh, I think so." The group of riders ambled down to the bottom of the hill.

We halted, in a loose queue, and Niamh turned to me. "Want to jump?"

"Yeah," I said.

Simple. No trying to wrap me in cotton wool, no trying to save me from myself. You want to jump? Yeah? Okay. You don't? Okay, too. No fuss. Yes or no. Take your pick, either one is fine. As simple as that.

There was always a moment in The Three Jump Field when I freaked out, when Delilah trotted for only one beat, and then burst into the canter. This time I straightened her up, and off we went, heading to the tire jump, and I was free, like that fall had never happened, and I tapped her with my crop, and we soared over the tires, then cleared the plank, and then—

There were horses turned out, and there was one in our line to the log, not by much, we could have cut around him, but I couldn't decide what to do. I decided fuck it, can't risk it—I didn't know the horse that was in the way, didn't know how he'd react—so we gently cantered away from the log, the infamous log, and headed back to join the group.

A decision not to do something is, in fact, a decision.

We went again: tires, plank, and this time, the obstructive horse was gone, and I turned us toward the log, and I felt Delilah start to back off. Aha! She didn't like the log, either! But we were already committed to the approach, so I tapped her again with my crop, gently, a small reminder, and I let her jump it at her own pace.

And over we went!

We did it: we communicated, we listened to each other, and we jumped that dreaded log, and everything I'd read in the books was true.

Which books? All the books. Every book about horses, every book about relationships, every book with twelve steps, every book about codependency. In fact, I wouldn't swear that there wasn't a spiritually healing message to be found in all the books about horse breeding, and equine feed, and tack.

What were they right about? That people-pleasing—or pony-pleasing—is a guaranteed foolproof way to weave yourself into a doormat. That not telling the truth hurts, and can get you hurt. That the constant shuffling of boundaries is unsafe—physically, mentally, and emotionally. That all of the above combine to make a person unbelievable (as in, "Why should I feel threatened when you say you're going to leave, when you never, ever do?"). That it doesn't feel like love anymore when it's a power struggle.

And that you are stuck because all the previous bad outcomes have conglomerated into an inflexible perception: You can't do anything, you will lose, you will fail, you will be shamed. There is only so much peace and joy and comfort you are entitled to. *This* is all you deserve. *This* will never get better.

It will never get better if you think that in order to change, it must all change at once. You cannot leave for your own good and also see to the good of the person you are leaving. You cannot live your truth without telling it. You cannot know what the outcome will be.

You can protect yourself from the actions of others. You can go up to the little room in the house that has been set aside as an office/studio, plug in an audiobook by Louise Hay, and start making necklaces—occupational therapy for the recovering control freak. The beads, inanimate objects, don't object to being strung, and something pretty comes out of it in the end. You can breathe and breathe and breathe. You can repeat, over and over, affirmations that seem trite and foolish. And all the while, downstairs, there is either the enraged slamming of pots and pans and doors or (worse) an ominous silence out of which anything could erupt. But you have begun. You have done one thing. You have made one necklace. You have detached, even if only for an hour.

The Saturday that I woke, sweating with fear and afraid to ride Maverick, I got up, got out of bed, and went to the barn. I got my boots and back protector out of my locker, put them on. I took my emotional temperature: still fluttery in the belly, still chilly in the veins.

I decided to head down to the outdoor ring to watch the lesson in progress. I thought maybe I'd see how Maverick was going for someone else, see how I reacted to his actions while I was still safely on the ground...except he wasn't there.

I'd become friendly with several of the "pony moms," and the one named Deirdre was watching her daughter's lesson. She asked me how my riding was going, and which horse I was going to take that day.

"I've been riding Maverick lately," I said, poking at a rock with my crop. "But honestly, I feel a little afraid today."

"My daughter is like that every now and again," Deirdre said. "When I used to ride myself, I'd get that fear."

"The horse fear," I confirmed.

"Riding is dangerous; we know it is," she went on. "But sometimes it just hits you, what could happen, if you fall the wrong way, or the horse runs off on you..."

"Sometimes I'm afraid I'm going to scare myself out of doing it altogether," I admitted. "Or that I'm not trying hard enough. Like I should keep going with Maverick, but..."

"Ah, sure, you might like a new horse better." Which was a lovely, positive mom-type thing to say. We turned our attention back to the lesson."Oh, now, that's high," Deirdre commented. The instructor had put the last fence in a grid up to three feet. The daughter took it with ease on a speedy little piebald that was one of the highly-sought ponies.

"She's going well on him," I observed.

"They had a terrible winter," Deirdre said. "She was getting frustrated but wouldn't hear a word about changing. It's up to her to decide, whether she wants to change the pony she rides or not."

"Builds character," I said. This was true: The pony girls were friendly, self-assured; they walked around the barn like they owned it and were always up for a chat, even with a grown up who was only a beginner.

"It does, and I'm hoping it'll keep her off the partying and boys for another four years at least!"

"You should take it up again yourself," I said.

"Oh, God!" She laughed. "I'm not as brave as you."

I *could* be brave. I *would* be. I would say I wasn't riding Maverick that day. I was a grownup, even if I was a beginner, and I was paying for these lessons, so if I wasn't feeling right about riding him, then I would say so.

I made my way back up to the stable where I found several of my lessonmates already mounted...and someone else was on Maverick.

Well, shit.

I took Cathal, we had our best jumping lesson to date, and all the way home on the bus, I pondered the things that happen that are out of my control.

CHAPTER FIVE

CONTROL

I was pretty sure I wasn't going to like dressage. Not that I'd ever done it, but it certainly didn't appear to be as sexy as jumping, or as thrilling as that daydream about cantering through an open field into the sunset. Dressage seemed to be the very thing that made riding "posh." Fancy clothes, fancy music, fancy horse; white gloves, white breeches and high-stepping, dancing movements. This was everything "equestrian" that was utterly out of my realm, remote, beyond my capacity as a novice, school-horse rider.

Then I had the opportunity to watch some pony girls practice dressage moves in preparation for a competition. The rider had to get the horse to do things at specific places in the arena, without looking like she was doing anything: for example, she had to make it look as though the horse just up and decided to canter, and then equally as spontaneously decided to stop. The specific places were marked by those ubiquitous letters on the walls, and until that moment I had no idea that this was their true purpose. I watched and learned, but it still seemed tedious and dull, and it didn't appeal to me at all.

Then I got my hands on a sample "test," which gave you the assigned movements you were to perform, as well as where and when, and lo and behold, it was a list—very simple, appropriate for beginners, and the first few elements were:

1) A: Enter in working trot, proceed down the center line without halting and turn right at C.
2) CMB: Working trot; circle right twenty meters diameter at B.
3) BFAKE: Working trot.
4) E: Turn right; B: Turn left.
5) B: Working trot; circle left twenty meters diameter at E.

There were fourteen items, every move executed in both directions, and a salute—a bow of the head and a flourish of the right arm—at the end.

My first crack at this was in a lesson, two riders at a time, one after the other, rather than doing it by ourselves with a judge giving us marks. I would have liked to have tried it alone, but even though I'd thought I had it memorized, I couldn't remember all of it. Neither could anyone else. Niamh reminded us that *All King Edward's Horses Carried Many Brave Fools,* and we all followed her directions called from the ground, changing the rein from F (Fools) to H (Horses) on the long diagonal and then cantering in a circle from B (Brave) to E (Edward)—and then Maverick decided to pelt around in ever decreasing circles, trying to chuck me off.

He did not chuck me off. He was laying on the blistering speed, and we ran into the center of the arena, which (needless to say) was not one of the movements in the test, but we eventually got through it, and ended with the halt and salute in relief.

I wanted to try it again, though, immediately upon finishing. I wondered how much preparation it required to actually remember every move while managing your horse, getting him or her perfectly into the corners, and achieving the correct transition directly at the appropriate letter. Dressage was actually hard.

It required good horsemanship, intelligence, forethought, mental toughness, and enough skill to not betray any movement of the hands and seat that might telegraph the message meant for the horse to those watching.

Controlling something without anyone suspecting that's what I was doing? That was codependent crack! Crack and meth, rolled into one, with a cocaine chaser. It was my drug of choice: being perceived as cool, calm, and collected, running around, putting out metaphorical fires, sometimes putting them out before they'd even had a chance to blaze up, and sometimes creating the conflagration out of nothing so that I'd be able to demonstrate my prowess at managing the flames.

I loved managing things. And I loved lists. The best way I knew how to manage my life was with lists. When it came time to move the Long Distance Relationship into a No Distance Relationship, lists played a major part. We were going to live together in Ireland? I made a list of the things I had to do to make it work. And for good measure, I made a list of the stuff he needed to do, too. Bullet points and everything.

Lists were great: They were practical, and they showcased my ability to do the things I said I was going to do. They were a means of corralling my wayward thoughts and emotions. As they continued to play a large part in my marriage, they were also concrete ways to cover up abstract fears and worries.

The first item on one of my old lists might be:

1) Find out about getting a landline.

I was paying the bill for his mobile phone, and it was getting expensive. If I got a landline in his name, with the monthly payment drawing automatically from his account, wouldn't that solve the problem?

The benefits of doing this spawned a secondary list:

1) I am less resentful now that I'm not paying his mobile phone bill. The fact that he is responsible for managing a direct debit for something makes me feel better.
2) Now I have two numbers to call, to check up on him and see where he is and what he is doing.

I don't remember buying Melody Beattie's book *Codependent No More*, and I don't remember the first time I read it. I don't remember reading it the second time, either. The third time I read it, I wrote out what she suggested was a good distillation of the issues involved in codependency: "A codependent person is one who has let another person's behavior affect him or her, and who is obsessed with controlling that person's behavior."

When I read the book yet again, I came across that scrap of paper (tucked away in the book itself, hidden, not very helpful as an aid to remembering its message). When I looked at the handwriting, I began to feel breathless. *It* was breathless. It rushed across the torn sheet, struggling to anchor itself to the lines. There was an urgency there that didn't have to do with escape...I could feel the cursive yearning toward a solution to pain, fear, madness. I felt it dragging me forward with it, whether I liked it or not.

I didn't remember writing those words, but in less than a heartbeat, in less time than it took to read them, I once again felt the effects of a terrible cocktail of despair, resolve, fury, hope, and futility. I understood what the passage meant, beyond grammar and semantics, and I hated that knowing. I hated it with everything I was, every bone, every muscle, every cell in my body. There I was, again imperfect. How could I fix everything if I wasn't perfect? I read that book dutifully, three times, before registering its tagline the fourth time round: *How to Stop Controlling Others and Start Caring for Yourself.*

In my marriage, I didn't see my actions as controlling, even though I was accused of being so, regularly. I was used to being in charge of things, of staying ahead of the curve, of anticipating problems and offering solutions at the appropriate times.

I had plenty to keep me occupied in the beginning of The Relationship, and the long distance aspect was the perfect breeding ground into which I sowed the seeds of my neuroses and cultivated them. Anxiety, low self-esteem, distrust...it was amazing I didn't move back to the States to ensure the marriage continued. He had uprooted himself to join me, and therefore he had the biggest chip in the ongoing bargaining process. Such a chip would have been wasted on me had I had it, for I would never have used it—martyrdom is another symptom of codependency.

I was okay with friends or when I was alone, because I didn't have the same sort of expectations of them, and I understood solitude; there was nothing about it I needed to map out. If I was by myself, there was nothing to fix but me, and I could put that off forever. If I was with friends, and something uncomfortable came up, I could just go home and let space and time do its work. But there was no space and no time in my marriage, no present tense. It was all about what happened before and what would happen tomorrow. We had to endlessly revisit the past and worry about the future. There was no *now.*

"Now" was a problem, anyway. You couldn't do anything about now, you could only live through it. Now just happened, and you couldn't hedge your bets against it, you could only "be." There was no control regarding now: you couldn't orchestrate it or anticipate it, because it already "was." Nothing frightened me as much as being out of control. But by getting myself in a situation in which I was constantly on the alert, I had enough drama to keep me occupied for weeks and months and years. For the rest of my life. Forever and ever, establishing myself, once and for all, as the good, level-headed one, the one upon whose shoulders the well-being of the world rested. Onward I went, taking care of business, making things happen, fixing, fixing, fixing, covering up, fudging, rationalizing, and outright lying because if I didn't...

I didn't know what would happen if I didn't, and that scared me to death.

Nothing is as scary as feeling like a horse is out of control. Nothing feels as terrifying as a horse going too fast; nothing is as tense as the anticipation of a horse freaking out at a cartwheeling snack packet; nothing makes one feel as helpless as being unable to make a horse stop.

When a horse does something he is not supposed to do, the rider learns to recognize it within a stride, and the instructor immediately begins instructing, but...it is so hard to hear when the horse you are on is racing around the arena at top speed, if not impossible, because your brain just freezes up. So now the horse is in flight, the rider is in freeze, and it feels like the racing around will never end, or that there is only one way it *will* end—and that is with you flat on your back.

To complicate matters, your natural reactions are usually bad ones. Instinctively, you want to lean forward, gripping with your legs, and even more sensibly, you want to grab the reins and hold on tight. However, leaning forward makes the horse go faster; clenching with your legs makes the horse go faster; pulling on the reins makes the horse raise his head, and yes, quite possibly, go faster—or possibly rear. All the instinctive, defensive postures—curling up into a ball, holding on for dear life—are incorrect. All the responses that are counterintuitive are correct: Lean back. Close your legs but don't clamp. Lower your hands. The horse will stop.

Ah, Maverick. Every time I mastered one of his cunning little tricks, he pulled another out of the bag. As noted, he was known to stop, dead, before he would canter. And he wouldn't just stand there but would start to buck, or walk backward, or both. I would be enjoined from the ground: "Get after him," "Tap him on the bum with the crop," "Squeeze with your legs," "Keep the contact" (but not so much that he commences walking backward again). Or, "Sit back!" they would say when I couldn't get him to stop. Instructions would issue thick and fast, but in these moments I felt stunned and numb, my face frozen in a mask of confoundedness.

Something would eventually change, usually because Maverick decided he was done either not cantering or cantering, or I'd give up and let go. The lesson, interrupted by the shenanigans, would continue, and I'd apologize over and over for holding things up. I'd leave, berating myself for riding a horse that wouldn't listen to me, that did his best to make me look like a fool. I wanted to give up on this crazy horse that was out to get me, but I kept trying and trying and trying, because that was what I did.

There was one particular maneuver Mav pulled that drove me completely and utterly nuts: He did something my instructor called "falling in," meaning that he dropped his inside shoulder when going in a twenty-meter circle. I was able to manage this in the trot, but in the canter—or worse, after a fence?—it was a nightmare. My balance would be completely thrown out of whack, and he would charge ahead, cutting to the inside.

That's when I would fall.

117

Anticipating Maverick's deception messed with my head, and often all I'd do the whole lesson was worry about him: What was he going to do wrong? What did I need to do to prevent him from doing it? *Could* I do anything to prevent it? Off we'd go again, taking our turn to canter around the arena, and all of a sudden he'd be charging and falling in and I wouldn't be able get him back on the literal track. There was an essential *something* that was missing, and I didn't know what it was.

And then I learned about the belly-button thing.

I had different kinds of lessons at the different places I rode. At the barn where I racked up two of my falls, I was that annoying "randomer" who paid for a lesson, who the instructor didn't know and had to assess, and who was given one of the horses that would never be given to a regular rider at the barn, because they were sour or dead to the leg or both.

At my regular lesson stable, I got to do loads of jumping, and go go go go, which was exhilarating.

And then there was the third place I went to ride, where it was all about form and control. This was good, because I was missing some details, some of the finer points that I had read about in the horse books. I knew I was getting into bad habits riding Maverick: My hands were getting heavy, I was leaning on his mouth, and since I was relying on my hands, my legs weren't getting strong enough to guide him. I wanted to slow down a bit, take things step by step, gain some confidence, some finesse. It was at the third barn where I rode twenty-meter circles at the walk for half an hour. So, yeah—loads of time devoted to doing the littlest things.

I talked about Maverick all the time to anyone who would listen, and so one of the instructors at the third barn got an earful. There I was, confidently guiding Joxer around the arena, complaining about Maverick. And that's when I was taught the belly-button thing.

The belly-button thing is this: If you are on the right rein, you shift your pelvis the slightest bit so that your belly button is in line with the horse's right ear. Same on the left, only opposite. What this action does is move your seat slightly so there is slightly more weight in your outside stirrup, and it also makes it easier for you to keep your inside leg on the girth. Keeping more pressure on the inside of the horse's body causes him to move away from it; by having that extra bit of weight on the outside, it means he can't start drifting. The horse is encouraged to stay balanced and the rider is back in control.

I was told that the next time Maverick started to fall in, I should do the belly-button thing, even if my body felt like it was the wrong thing to do, as it would throw his balance off just enough to make him stop dropping his shoulder. If he ignored me when I did the belly-button thing, he'd fall over. But, luckily for me, he would sense that he was about to fall over and would correct himself to prevent it from happening.

Uh, okay.

Or maybe he would just fall over and *BOOM!* Leg under a thousand pounds of horse.

Thanks for nothing, belly-button thing.

I don't remember much from my first Al-Anon meeting, but I'll never forget it. Off I went, seething and resentful—I mean, why did I have to go and do happy-clappy twelve-step shit? All those years in New York, I'd successfully avoided what seemed to be a residential requirement to go to some support group or other. Not me, thanks. I could cope with everything that city dished out; I didn't need to sit around, most likely in a circle, thanking people for sharing, doling out earnest hugs.

As far as I knew, Al-Anon members were a bunch of people who had to learn how to stop the addicts in their lives from being addicts. In all my book-buying, Internet-surfing fervor, I didn't even bother looking into the group's mission and theories. I guess I really didn't want to know.

Grumbling crossly to myself, slipping sideways into the building like a criminal, I trudged my way up three flights of stairs to the meeting. I was greeted warmly by the women who were present, and I waited to be interrogated as to my qualifications for entry, my reasons for being there, for everything.

I was not. I was left to sit, in the quiet, unbothered, until the meeting began.

I scanned the banner that hung on the wall, touting the famous twelve steps. Right, I thought, immediately making it a list to check off. A step a week for twelve weeks. I reckoned I'd be outta there in three months.

People began sharing, and I felt like a hand had reached into my chest and squeezed my heart. They laughed, and I wondered, How can they laugh? They are living a nightmare! People hugged me at the end, and I don't know how I didn't sink to the floor in a heap. They told me that, as a new member, I was the most important person in the room that day, and even though I was certain that my membership was going to be of very short duration, well, it touched me.

I do remember, clearly, calling my husband after I left the meeting, saying, "Well, I just left that meeting." Listening to his silence. And then, "It was fine. The people seemed nice."

What I was really thinking was: See? I said I would do this, even if I don't have to. I said I would do this bullshit twelve-step garbage because I am committed to making *you* better. I went, even though *I* don't need this. So now what are *you* gonna do about it?

His response to what I said, but probably equally to what I was thinking, was: "Yeah? So?"

Subtext: "That's not my shit."

He was absolutely correct. It was entirely *my* shit. It would take me years to understand that.

I went to one meeting a week and considered myself a candidate for sainthood. I bought an Al-Anon book and dutifully read the page-a-day, and didn't let on, even to myself, the way in which my life was mirrored in those pages. It made me want to shake and cower and scream and rip the book into tiny pieces. And yet, I made friends In The Rooms (and started to use phrases like "In The Rooms," which is total twelve-step-speak), and began to go to another meeting during the week. And yet, taking the suggested behaviors outside of The Rooms proved to be something else altogether. I would try one little thing, maybe I would "let go and let God," but God certainly wasn't in any rush to sort things out for me, so in I would go again, doing the same things I'd always done, fixing, managing, fudging, whatever I thought it took to make a change.

Nothing changed, and I kept at it and kept at it. And I'd talk about it and talk about it in meetings, and while nobody was telling me I was wasting my time, neither did they tell me to talk about something else, or that what I was saying was pointless; they only told me to keep working at the steps, to have faith in The Program. It seemed like it was all an absolute waste of time. I still had no idea how to stop doing the things I wasn't supposed to do. It was ridiculous! Pointless! All these women (mainly women), sitting around in a room, talking about detachment and serenity and "letting go, letting God."

For God's sake, *what?* Or rather, *who?* God who? Seriously? I considered myself spiritual, but I didn't think I actually believed in God. As far as I could tell, God certainly didn't understand me, so how was I supposed to understand God? God didn't understand that when I asked for help, I expected help. I used to routinely go to a church off Grafton Street and light a candle at the feet of the Infant of Prague. I didn't know anything about the Infant of Prague, but I felt calm there, in the little side chapel, usually on my own, the better to weep behind my sunglasses and pray, over and over, *Fix it, fix it, fix it, please fix it.* Fix him. Fix the whole mess of a marriage so that we could move forward together, so that all this other shit would just get out of the way, so that we could be better together.

Stubborn, I kept going to those meetings, without the slightest bit of confidence that anything was going to come of it. I also kept reading books, and trying to find all the answers I wanted to find in them. I avoided the codependency canon, except for Beattie. And there were bits in her book that I dodged as well. For example, there was a list of typical codependent behaviors at the beginning of a chapter entitled, "Set Yourself Free," a list that I was almost unable to read in its entirety:

> We nag; lecture; scream; holler; cry; beg; bribe; coerce,
> hover over; protect; accuse; chase after; run away from;
> try to talk to; try to talk out of, chase after; run away
> from; attempt to induce guilt in, seduce, entrap; check
> on; demonstrate how much we've been hurt...pray for
> miracles; pay for miracles; go to places we don't want to
> go; stay nearby; supervise; dictate, command; complain;
> write letters about; write letters for; stay home and
> wait for; go out and look for; call all over looking for...
> settle issues once and for all; settle them again; punish;
> reward; almost give up on; then try even harder...[1]

So it's not just me, then? I'm not the only one who is trying to control? Control *what*?

Good question.

Control everything. Control what happened when it happened, control something so that something else didn't happen. Do everything for someone else he could actually do for himself, except he didn't do it when I wanted it done.

If A didn't happen, then what about B? And forget about C—we'd never get there. The goals of a partnership, from home to children to retirement, were slipping like sand through an hourglass. There wasn't enough time, and if I didn't keep the list at the forefront of my mind, I'd forget what the point of it all was.

I transgressed about every boundary known to humankind. I progressed beyond searching through pockets, and when he was zoned out, I took to scrolling through text messages, seeing if he left his email open, holding letters up to the light. I lived that horrible list in Beattie's book, every day, in some way, shape, or form, and it didn't help that I knew that I was in the wrong. (Although it did allow me the bonus round of feeling crushed by guilt, which inflamed my persecution complex, so there was that. That was a buzz.)

I tried to try. I said, "I won't be paying all the bills anymore," and thought I meant it. In truth, I couldn't make sense of how to actually stick to such a statement; it was utterly out of my realm. Slowly, at a glacial pace, I began to try to employ parameters of some stripe, ones that had only to do with my own behavior. That's what they kept saying in The Rooms: "We can only be responsible for our own behavior."

I failed. I overlooked the telltale signs The Cycle was starting again, and thought about quitting The Program. I needed to find the answer somewhere else, in a place where somebody was going to tell me exactly what I had to do, and when, and how.

After I gave it a chance, I found that I really liked dressage. I liked that I didn't memorize the pattern of movements only with my mind, but my body as well. I imagined the moves sinking into my muscles, every time I rode them. I was beginning to contain them, and it felt good, because I wasn't doing it all by myself. I had to communicate—directly, simply, and clearly—to the horse.

The horses seemed to really like dressage, too. Maybe even love it. It was like they knew it was different: It wasn't that I insisted they go all the way to K before turning to change the rein, just to be annoying. It was like they were aware this wasn't just rote-lesson-stuff, but that there was greater purpose to my riding, and it seemed like they were taking my aids more seriously.

Like that time Delilah and I practiced a Prix Caprilli test—dressage with jumps—and after the jump at B, we were supposed to gradually shift over toward the track and end up at M. As the mare was so stiff, this seemed to me something we'd never achieve, but I put my inside leg on the girth and over we shifted, smoothly and easily, as if we did such a thing every day. This was stunning and miraculous, as Delilah rarely did any-thing even when you asked nicely for it, without an argument. (I once watched her in what was a beginner's class. When the riders were instructed to walk around on the left rein, I watched Delilah stare off into the middle distance as her rider ineffec-tually tapped at the mare's sides with reluctant heels. They're going nowhere fast, I thought as I left the arena, and marveled at how the application of attitude was as essential as the application of aids.)

Doing dressage put me in an extraordinary state of mind. I wasn't obsessing about the horse, about what he might take into his head to do next because I knew *exactly* what we were going to do next. I was focused on what I needed to do, which was hit the track at M, canter at C, circle at A. Because I was minding myself, and thinking for myself and myself alone, I could communicate more clearly and simply with the horse.

Yes, that outside leg sliding back just a heartbeat before C means canter, Delilah.

And so she did.

I found that when I was fully engaged in keeping my mind on my own business, the horse was able to go about his business, and as a result, we made a coherent, cohesive team. The presto-chango quality of the different requests at each letter kept the horse's mind engaged, and the fact that I had to be very quiet about making those requests, well, that was really good for me.

Note I said "requests," not "demands." A quote from Carl Jung comes to mind, one that says that opposite of love is not hate, but the will to power. At one stage, I was not feelin' the love where Mav was concerned; after about a year of stonewalling on his part, I was getting tired of the struggle and couldn't see a way forward, except perhaps on the back of another horse.

"Sue, you're down for Maverick," Emily said, reading the list, on the night I'd decided I'd had enough. Someone else had been assigned Delilah, and I made the mistake of telling Emily that Mav and I'd had a (typically) difficult experience in the previous lesson. Emily brooked no resistance to reengaging with a challenging mount, and I suppose that was to the good, as it was confidence-building and all that...right?

Where did it cross the line, though, into irreparability? Was there room for compromise, for example? When Maverick would not stay in trot, I would do as I was told and get after him, knowing he would buck, knowing I would wobble, knowing we would eventually go, but at what cost? We both ended up ticked off at each other, both of us engaging in a power struggle, and all the love going down the drain.

Emily allowed me to allow Maverick to walk when the horse and rider in front of us started to canter, rather than insisting he stay in trot. It worked wonderfully well: when it was our turn, he moved flawlessly up into the trot, and then immediately picked up the canter as I asked. So, at least with Emily, there *was* room for negotiation and compromise. Another instructor might not be so magnanimous; in fact, I knew of one or two who would not allow that leniency. But I didn't think I had that much to prove. (Did I?) I'd learned that given the choice between a power struggle and a graceful withdrawal, I'd just as soon step away, thanks. Otherwise nobody wins, at the end of the day.

I wished I'd known this earlier. See, I thought Husband and I had crafted a compromise every time we made it out of The Cycle and promised to be better: We would both recover, that is, he would stop misusing substances and I would stop being a lunatic. But according to my Oxford Dictionary, compromise also meant "the acceptance of standards that are lower than is desirable." I accepted that I went to meetings—after deciding not to quit after all—and decided that was enough. It wasn't, though, because nothing was changing, and the meetings were just a straw man, a blind, more wishful thinking.

It became apparent, toward the end of my ability to sustain my activities as a rampant codependent, that the marriage *was* a power struggle, and that even though I was the overt controller, I was in fact being controlled both by his actions and by his lack of action-taking. I had to figure out how to not react to his behavior, to mind my own business. I had to figure out how to change my own behavior.

I had to figure out how to stop.

Two lesson groups were stuffed into the indoor arena due to bad weather. Even though there were eleven of us, adults and children, plus an equal number of horses, we mostly managed to remain contained...except for one mare, Bounty, who was showing her youth and freshness by skitting about the place. I kept a prudent distance: we were right behind them, and Maverick habitually liked to get up-close-and-personal with the lead horse.

We all began trotting in a twenty-meter circle, in which lay two sets of poles to go over: one set of three on the track side of the circle, and another set at X, both of which added negotiation in the curve. Bounty didn't like this. She jigged over the poles as though they were on fire, and took every approach to them as if it was her last action as a living, breathing creature.

On one such approach—one in which, in fairness, we were indeed a bit too close to her—she got spooked, and so Mav got spooked, and he leaped and jittered out of the line and started to buck and I...

...I sat back.

No one yelled at me to sit back. I just felt my pelvis tuck in—ah! He stopped bucking. I walked him in a circle, and rejoined the group.

In that moment, there was awareness: I felt it deep in my muscles with some input from my mind, but not much. I didn't tell myself, Sit back! I just...did it, and even gave Maverick a squeeze to keep him moving forward. As quickly, quietly, and simply as that, I had a major breakthrough.

It takes time to process something intellectually about riding horses. Since much of it is counterintuitive, it's a struggle to believe, in your mind, that sitting back is actually safer than curling up in a ball on the horse's neck. I believe it in my mind, now, because I did it in my body, and having done it a sufficient number of times since, I rarely consciously call upon this movement as a solution: it's just there, and I do it.

That sort of success built on itself. At another point in time, Maverick had been off work for a good while. He was back on the job and I had him for my Tuesday-night lesson. On the walk from the barn to the indoor, I could tell by his step that he was very fresh. I got up there, and the lesson began, and...

...I just rode. I could feel his fizz up through the reins as he leaned on the bit and tried to go go go, and I could feel it in my bum, of course. He was pulling and leaning and buzzing and bucking, and I...I just rode.

When we cantered, he got completely spooked at the door for no reason (sometimes there is a reason, but this time, there wasn't). I wobbled for a second and then sat back, circled him back onto the track, and started over.

We moved on to canter over poles, and he decided to jump them the first time. So I sat back, and we tried it again.

He wasn't getting the five strides we wanted in between the poles, so Niamh said to "shorten him up," and I pretty much knew what that meant. I pinched up my buttocks—like I was pulling his gait up through my spine or something—and he totally responded.

As we were leaving the indoor at the end of the lesson, I said to Niamh, "You know, a year ago, two years ago, I would have been frozen during a lesson like that." Not because of the physical challenge, but because of my fear of being out of control. But sometimes there are days when you forget to be afraid. On those days, you maybe start to trust yourself, trust your instincts, and not worry so much. On those days, even though bad things have happened in the past, maybe they aren't going to happen again, because you've decided to do something differently. You've decided to change.

Sitting upstairs in the studio, beading my necklace, I was slowly creating my own experience of detachment. I was amazed at myself for being able to concentrate; I also felt nervous and defiant. Also: hopeful that my experiment would fail, so I could prove Al-Anon wrong, but equally hopeful that it would work, because nothing else was working, and something had to work... soon. I sat there, listening to Louise Hay as I felt the beads in my fingers, guided them onto the string, breathing, "letting go and letting God."

The front door would slam, and I sat still, and I breathed, working another bead onto the string. And I suppose...I suppose I prayed. It felt like a prayer, this breathing, in and out; creating the necklace seemed like a devotional act, and all the while Louise Hay gently exhorted me through the earbuds, telling me it would all be okay:

> All is well. Everything is working out for my highest good. Out of this situation only good will come. I am safe.

While I was engaged in crafting jewelry, I couldn't fan flames in order to put them out. I couldn't contribute to a crisis that actually needed my contribution for it to be a crisis in the first place. When I didn't engage in trouble-making, there was nothing to blow up in my face, and by the time the situation did implode and explode and 'plode in every manner of 'plosion, I had learned something: I had learned that a little detachment didn't kill anybody. I learned that I had enough self-respect to do that detaching in the first place. I learned that I could take care of myself. I could make decisions that were for my highest good.

I learned the value of *responding* rather than *reacting*. I was not only detaching from the behavior of another, I was also detaching from all evidence of previous outcomes. In fact, that evidence was incomplete, because all I had ever done was the same thing over and over. By doing a new thing—nothing—I learned that all I could control, in any given situation, ever, was my own response to that event. The only thing I could do was take some time to sit with that reaction, and then make a choice as to what to do from there. I was giving myself the opportunity to gain evidence that there *could* be a better outcome, and the more proof I got, the easier it was to believe that good things would continue to happen.

While there were still lists organizing the various parts of my life, they began to relate to things that were entirely my responsibility and within my remit. My lists didn't have anything to do with managing things so that everything stayed status quo; I no longer made lists that had to do with the things someone else had to change about his behavior, and I was always delighted to find a list made by someone else, like the list of codependent behaviors in Beattie's book, that was cogent and useful.

The more I trusted my riding instructors, the better I did from lesson to lesson, from day to day. The thing with horses, though, and relationships, too, was to not take anything for granted. The situation was constantly evolving, all sorts of influences were always being felt, and it helped to stay a little detached from all outcomes. Detachment sounded good—did that mean I wouldn't have to feel bad ever again?

CHAPTER SIX

FEEL

I don't even know how I can express the degree to which I thoroughly and unequivocally hated feelings—yes, even the enjoyable ones...maybe especially those. That first crush buzz? It wasn't going to last. As wonderful as that new relationship fervor was, it could face extinction at any moment. The bad feelings were a source of constant anxiety, and the good ones were anxiously awaited, and then just as anxiously experienced, because I knew exactly when they were going to take a turn for the worse. Sometimes, feeling bad was actually preferable: Why bother enjoying myself? It was only going to go to shit.

Perhaps it was all about the anxiety, really: nothing like being worried about being worried, or feeling sad that there was the potential for sadness in my heart.

The anxiety served to distance me from feeling actual feelings because, to me, feelings represented a vortex of reaction and overreaction that was exhausting and demoralizing. It became easier, throughout my childhood and the majority of my life, to just keep them in control, to scribble them out in a series of journals, or blurt them out occasionally to trusted friends. The latter, though, was only a last resort, because there was a front to be maintained—I was meant to be unflappable.

I would get lost in the anxiety so that it wrung me out, until, boneless and beaten, I would stop feeling the thing that inspired the anxiety and go back to a neutral place. It was exhausting to have feelings because I couldn't do anything with them. I couldn't express myself, I couldn't reasonably articulate what I was experiencing, because it might make my husband feel bad, and who knew what that might inspire. So I had to have all the feelings, all by myself.

In *Codependent No More* there is an entire chapter on feelings. When I picked it up for the fourth time, I was surprised to find my copy was curiously bereft of the underlinings and dog-eared corners that are standard practice when I want something to jump out at me, should I consult the book in the future. Clearly, I did not want anything from this book jumping out at me. Particularly the section exploring a strange phenomenon, which I surely wasn't ready to take on board back then, and didn't want to be redirected toward: the fact that our feelings are our own responsibility.

> People might help us feel, but they don't make us feel. People also cannot change the way we feel. Only we can do that. Furthermore, we are not responsible for anyone else's feelings, although we are responsible for choosing to be considerate of people's feelings. Responsible people choose to do that, at times. However, most codependents choose to overdo that. We need to be considerate of our feelings, too. Our feelings are reactions to life's circumstances. Thus, etiquette requires that when you discuss a feeling with someone, you say, "I feel such and such when you do such and such because..." not "You made me feel..." [2]

This concept seemed impossible for me to grasp. You can be sure I had a list of the reasons why:

132

1) How could it be that my husband wasn't responsible for how I was feeling? Didn't he just do the thing that made me feel something?
2) The notion that I could actually say in language what I felt, other than "shitty" was...frankly, there was no notion that I could do that.
3) What difference would it make if I started talking about how I felt? It wasn't like I was going to be heard.

I had made threats at times, in the "things had better change around here or else" vein, but I never actually followed through, so why should he believe anything I said? Why should I believe myself? I sighed and sulked my way around the house because I didn't know any other way of showing that I was upset, or annoyed, or scared. It was beyond my capacity to "own" my feelings because I didn't *want* to own them...I just wanted them to go away.

It eventually dawned on me that sighing and sulking, berating and nagging, doing things when I wasn't asked to do them, seething with resentment, and forcing what I thought were good solutions—none of it was working. Something was beginning to rumble underneath the surface, a mix of fear and grief that I was, at long last, getting the message. This was the way things were with this relationship, take it or leave it.

So I left it.

August of 2005. It had been a particularly bad Cycle. We'd been together for seven years, married for two. One night, I made the meal, and he sat nodding off in front of his plate, barely reacting when I started cleaning up and putting things away. Nothing, no conversation about the day, no "Thank you," no offer to help, no response at all—just a stumble up the stairs to bed. The next morning, a silent, ragey man made himself breakfast and proceeded to sit down in front of me and eat it. Afterward, he went into the living room and started doing sit-ups on the floor in front of the hearth.

I followed him, sat down in a chair facing him as he crunched up and down. Worked up the courage to speak.

Then I said, "This isn't working for me. I...I can't keep doing this."

One sit-up, another. "So?"

Wow.

"So...I don't know what to do about it. This situation."

One sit-up, two, three. "I'm busy; I'm working out."

Oh, man.

"I have to go to a press conference in town." I was now perched on the edge of the chair, not sure if I wanted to grab him and make him look at me or jump up and run. I sat, frozen, and forged ahead. "But I need to talk about this later."

Another sit-up, two. "I'm not moving out."

"I didn't say that we need to break up..." my hasty reply, "...but it's not working..."

"I'll move into the studio." One, two, three, four sit-ups, fast. *What?*

"What? And we'll live like roommates?"

One, two, three, four, more. "So what?"

"That's not going to work for me."

No response. I stood up, over him, still crunching: one, two, three, four, five more sit-ups.

I went upstairs, threw some clothes into a bag, and left. At the press conference, I saw a friend and asked if I could stay with her for a bit. It was the beginning of the end.

In two months, I would live in the bedsit as I made one more effort to save my marriage.

Ten months after that, I left him for good.

One way I liked to distance myself from the whole messy business of feelings was to try to make sense of them intellectually. I would read about, say, love or fear, and figure out what they were, in concrete terms, in terms of neural pathways and hormones.

Yes, this made me *feel* better.

There is a scientific explanation as to how falling in love works, how fear works, how memory works. Feeling, then, isn't much less autonomic than breathing, really. I'd always thought you don't have control over feelings because they happen in your brain, and isn't it true that we only use a small percentage of our gray matter? The brain is as remote as the moon, in a way, so good luck to anyone who wants to manage what goes on in there. But feelings are, in fact, biochemical and in our bodies as much as they are in our brains, if not more so. Feeling fear may result in a cold sweat and an increased heart rate. Feeling love can result in a hot sweat and an increased heart rate (and a complete inability to make proper decisions, even when faced with obvious solutions, even when past experience has taught you that your partner is rather adept at saying one thing and doing another). According to *Psychology Today*, "Experience is encoded in our brains as a web of fact and feeling. When a new experience calls up a similar pattern, it doesn't unleash just stored knowledge but also an emotional state of mind and a predisposition to respond in a certain way."

Emotions? Aren't they the same as feelings? Is emoting different from feeling? I found myself in a wormhole of conflicting meanings: Emotions are the things that lie behind the feelings. Feelings are reactions to emotions. "Emotions" is an umbrella term that covers actual situations and the way that we interpret them, while "feelings" are the responses to what the emotions decide the situations are.

Or, most tellingly, according to Walter Last in his online article "The World of Feeling and Emotions": "'Emotions'...are feelings or reactions about someone or something, and usually involving our ego. We are angry about someone, afraid of something, in love with someone. These emotions may be directly felt in the body or we may just react strongly with thoughts or verbal displays originating from our head."

Well, crap. If I was making stuff up in my head, including the way I felt, based on experiences that were mine and mine alone, then it was therefore true that no one could *make* me feel anything, and that this really was something I needed to become more responsible for. My "respond-ability" (as we'd say in my twelve-step program) was actually something I had some control over. In fact, it might be the only thing that I could get a handle on.

When you ride, you hold the reins in a very specific way. You slip the leather between the pinky and ring fingers of both hands, and with the reins running across the tops your palms (where they meet the base of your fingers), you hold them still by pressing your thumbs against the outsides of your index fingers. You hold on, to the correct degree. You have to keep your fingers closed, but not clenched. You feel a pressure on the ends of the reins where they meet the bit, which is in the horse's mouth. You feel weight. This is called *contact*, and it is one of the ways you communicate with the horse during the course of a ride. When you have "bad" contact, you spoil the horse's mouth. The result?

1) A horse that is resistant to the directions of the rider.
2) A horse that leans on the rider's hands because he can only respond to serious pressure.
3) A horse that is, as they say, "heavy on the forehand"—that is, he carries his weight in the shoulders rather than in the hindquarters.

In other words: Maverick.

All the things that drove me crazy about him were only exacerbated by my learning curve, which began at zero. I could understand, intellectually, all the things I'd read about keeping up a good contact, about how it was supposed to feel like I was holding bags of sugar in my hands (or a similar amount of weight). When I went to the market to try to get the feel of this in my body, *I got it*. I saw how it made sense...in the baking aisle in the grocery store. It had an element of allowance to it as well—that is, if I allowed one hand to feel heavier than the other, then that hand was going to drop. When I raised that hand back up, only as far as necessary to be back in balance, it felt good, and both hands—mentally, as well as physically—felt like they were the same weight.

Standing still, at my leisure in a supermarket, this was easy enough to correct. When it translated to the horse that seemed to want nothing more than to pull my arms out of their sockets, I lost all sense of the feeling. I was very conscious of how hard and heavy my hands were becoming on a horse, that my seat wasn't very stable, and that anything that I was learning, bad as well as good, was being burned into my hippocampus. When the day came and I stopped riding Maverick, I would have hands like vises and legs like lead. I needed to learn ways to correct my bad habits.

I found myself intrigued by a movement known as "natural horsemanship." Known as "horse whispering" to the general public, the practice involved employing a gentle approach to training horses, one focused on their psychological well-being as opposed to the force used in "breaking" them. It respected the natural instincts of the horse and sought to take fear and pain out of the learning process in order that the horse bonded more closely and authentically with his human partner.

It was a competitive field, and as far as I could tell through my reading, like any other walk of life, people mostly liked criticizing the theories and practices of others. The primary issue that all the books and websites on the subject agreed on, and which I already knew, was that it was up to the rider to set the proper tone of clear communication and authority when it came to her horse. I watched countless YouTube videos made by a variety of well-known, well-regarded, horse-whispery types who seemed to demonstrate that all you had to do was walk up to a horse, and he would drop his head and follow you around like a puppy. I considered numerous ladies, jumping picnic tables bareback, their horses kitted out with nothing but a bit of rope over their noses, and the riders without boots or helmets. That was not my ambition, by any means, and I didn't really learn anything from such displays, but there was a freedom there—and *that* was what I wanted. I didn't want to fight the whole time. I wanted to communicate cleanly and clearly and not cause harm to the horse or myself.

I found a barn—this one even farther away from where I lived than my home base with Delilah and Maverick and Cathal and company—that seemed to subscribe to such notions, and I booked a lesson. I didn't know what to expect; I certainly did not expect to be flinging myself around over picnic tables. I chatted with the instructor, Sheila, and the guy who was tacking up a horse named Jack, my mount for the hour. Sheila explained that we'd be taking the lesson slowly as it was unlikely, given my relative newness to horseback riding, that I would have ever ridden without a bit....

Without a bit?

Oh, shit.

I nodded as my interior monologue went absolutely berserk: no bit no bit no bit.

I led Jack into the indoor arena—an enormous, pristine, mirrors-at-all-the-strategic-points arena, with the now-familiar letters in their proper places on the walls—and did everything I usually do: got a block, grabbed rein and mane, got myself up there. Then I sat and listened as Sheila explained, in her own words, all the things I'd been reading about natural horsemanship since well before I'd ever even got up on a horse.

I thought, This could be cool.

As Sheila turned to walk away after my stirrups had been adjusted and the girth checked for appropriate tightness, Jack followed her, and I realized then that my seat and legs may just as well not have been there. We stopped, eventually, most likely due to his choice rather than my direction. I was reminded of my very first lesson, the one on Mercury, when I sat frozen and hyperventilating. This wasn't as fraught, but it sure as hell was as nervous-making.

I rode some of the worst circles of my life. At the trot, the sound of my ass hitting the leather reverberated around the arena as if it were mic'ed. I realized that I hadn't asserted myself with Jack from the get-go. It was confirmed that my hands needed a lot of work. It was glaringly apparent that my left side was weak.

It was also demonstrated that I *could* learn, and improve, and that when working toward being a better rider, I could absorb new concepts. Once I got used to it, I got better at it: I made turns that were predominantly directed from my seat; we had a brilliant trot on the right rein, and some really smooth and well-transitioned cantering.

I rode Maverick the next day, and my hands went back to shit, but you know what? I rode some of the best circles I'd ever ridden on him, because I let him know I was there from the start, and we cantered like the bejeezus because I felt secure in the saddle. I couldn't wait to go back for another bitless lesson, so I booked myself in for the next week.

The second one went somewhat differently.

I'd been on a variety of horses since I'd begun riding, but I hadn't yet encountered the kind of horse I'd been reading about— one that was sensitive to me, as a rider and as a person, that would demonstrate to me, in a holistic, yet no-nonsense way, how I needed to grow.

It wasn't all it was cracked up to be.

When I saw Marty in the holding pen, I knew I would be riding him this time, not Jack. An absolutely massive, skewbald, cobby giant with a chest the width of a Hyundai, he raised his head as I walked over to him, and we looked at each other. He sniffed my nose; I blew back. He set his chin on my shoulder; I thought, Okay. This could work.

And it did, if by "work" I meant the total exposure of one's faults and weaknesses.

There was an equine-assisted-learning class happening in one end of the indoor arena; several horses were at liberty, meaning they were free to wander around as they pleased, and all that separated us was a large ceiling-to-ground divider that resembled a gigantic mesh curtain. Two of the horses came over to check out Marty and me; one of them, feeling threatened by my big guy, lunged at the curtain, and the mesh shook and the rings that held it on its rod rattled, and Marty got spooked and hopped around a bit. I didn't fall off, but I got spooked too, especially as I was still trying to acclimate to the bitless bridle. His head went straight up, and I pushed with my seat, which freaked him out more. I lost my nerve and immediately wanted to get off.

So we walked that lesson, a lot, with one trot of about ten strides at the very end that wasn't complete rubbish, and I wanted Jack, but I was told that if I stayed at the barn, I wouldn't be getting him back. Marty would be my mount.

I wanted to pack it in, say thanks but no thanks...but then what? Didn't I want to learn how to ride properly? Did I merely want to be one in the legions of people who never transcend the kick-and-jerk school of equestrianism? No. I didn't want to be that person.

Sheila and I chatted as I led Marty back to his stall. The pushing-with-the-seat thing was what got us off on such a bad foot, she explained. My seat, along with my hands, needed to be quiet. I nodded and took that in, and then Sheila said, "You work too hard."

I reckoned that people had probably spent thousands on years of therapy (I knew I had) and never gotten as clear, concise, and as true a diagnosis as that. Yes. I worked too hard, tried too hard, had to be perfect, couldn't fail. This wasn't something that was readily apparent—unless you were riding a horse that ushered such a quality into the spotlight, or if you were in a relationship that did the same.

There was nobody to tell me that I worked too hard...until that lesson, that moment—and that was all it was. Those four words. Nothing else. No castigation, no details, no exhaustive inventory of the perils of working too hard, no punishing words. Just those four alone, left for me to do with them what I would.

What I did was:

1) I felt absolutely awful about myself: I'd screwed up; I was worthless.
2) I got angry. Why didn't she tell me to *stop* working too hard, if she thought I was working too hard?
3) I felt wrong for feeling angry, and got sad as a result.
4) I vowed I would never, ever go to ride in that stupid place again.
5) I decided I would be back there next week, and I'd show her!

I believe this constituted an "emotional reaction."

I was Googling something called "horse feel." I'd heard someone at one of the barns I rode at talking about "feel," and it sounded to me like another one of those ineffable qualities that equestrians had...and I wanted it.

But as I typed in variations of the phrase, I wasn't coming up with much. Or all I was getting was an expanding number of people who were not able to tell me, directly and clearly, how to go about getting it. I wanted it to be as prescriptive as all that sciencey-brain stuff was regarding feelings, but it was yet another example of equivocal horseperson-talk. If there was one way to do something, there were at least three optional approaches that didn't exactly negate each other.

It was like those conversations I'd had with Roisin at what I now considered my "home barn," when I was talking about whether or not to buy my own horse; when I was waffling between a mare or a gelding, and trying to decide if a horse who'd only hunted was a good choice for me. There was never a direct yes-or-no answer to any of the possibilities I'd mooted, and Roisin talked me in and out of every proposition, every single time.

This was not the way I approached solving regular-life problems, but it was beginning to make sense to me as regarded equines. You obviously wouldn't know what you were dealing with in a horse until you rode him, so to project a whole bunch of problems onto one, before you'd even met him, was a waste of time. You also had to keep your mind open, which was the essence of what Roisin was trying to convey, because the subtleties of how I'd communicate with a horse would vary. Here's Bill Dorrance via Leslie Desmond, a noted horsewoman herself, who acted as co-author for his book *True Horsemanship Through Feel* (Dorrance is considered to be one of the founders of the natural horsemanship movement):

> What a person has in his mind to present to the horse needs to be something that's possible for a horse to actually do. Then the person has to be able to understand it themselves, through feel, and apply it in a way that the horse can understand. This is difficult because no two horses are the same, and there's plenty of adjusting a person needs to figure on for this. Even if the picture they have is okay, when they handle a horse with more firmness than he needs, they'll get a wrong response nearly every time and think the horse is at fault. When that's their thinking, they're liable to just apply a lot more pressure on the horse—which really mixes him up. And from the horse's response, the person can get the idea that he doesn't want to do what they'd like him to do. This is correct in a way, but it's really just because the horse can't figure out what they want him to do, because he doesn't understand that pressure-feel they put on him in the first place. What makes this so bad is that those horses—I'll say most horses—would cooperate if they could only understand.[3]

I got that, intellectually and emotionally. But how did I make a horse understand? Probably by not trying to *make* him, first off. I had tried to *make* many things happen when it came to other creatures, not just four-legged ones, with little to show for it, so I did know it was not the best approach. But between my impatience, fear of looking bad, and the now-known-fact that I worked too hard, it was difficult to feel like I was making *any* progress as far as horses were concerned. Failing on a horse was so public—there was always someone watching the lesson (I watched others' lessons, too, as often as I could), and you were so high up off the ground, it was like you were failing center stage, in a spotlight. I felt that it was a huge risk for me to try the new barn, the new horses, and riding without a bit, but I wanted so much to be *a rider*, one who was effective on a horse—and effective *for* the horse. I watched others ride so perfectly, and I wondered how long it would take me to get there.

It's hard not to take it personally when you do badly on a horse. But taking everything personally is not really a good plan in life.

I was making some headway toward not taking Maverick so personally. One Tuesday night, we were having a fairly typical lesson in the outdoor arena, and things were mostly okay until I went to join the group behind Spuddie. It was only two strides, maybe three, but Mav belted for the line and sped to catch up to Spud, and I thought, Uh-oh.

Around and around we went, with my horse absolutely focused on running up Spuddie's ass. I sat back, massaging the bit, and the reins were so short that my fingers were practically in Mav's mouth. By the time it was our turn to canter, he was really fighting me, and I tapped him with my crop—and he bucked like he meant it.

Now, Maverick mainly bucked the way a child might stick out his tongue. Cheeky, and annoying, and somewhat disrespectful, it was easily corrected, and everybody moved on.

This time it was different. I was thrown fully forward, and a little to the right, and for a second I saw the arena fence and thought, Crap, there I go, over the fence, but I managed to haul myself upright, left stirrup lost. Maverick fulfilled the promise of his earlier gallopy strides, and took off. I heard Niamh call out, "Sit baaaaaaack," really gently, as if talking to a horse and not a flailing rider, and I sat baaaaaack and dropped my leg, massaging the bit some more—and then I lost the outside stirrup, panicked for two seconds, got the stirrup back, managed to bring him into canter at the short end of the arena, and then I transitioned down to trot and rejoined the rest of the lesson. We trotted, still arguing, while everyone else cantered their turn on the left, and just as we were about to change direction...

I pulled Maverick into the center of the ring and sat there. And then I got down. Something felt wrong. I felt like I was giving up, but Niamh said to put him away and get Cathal instead, no big deal.

"How was Tuesday?" Roisin asked as I got up on Maverick two days later in a private lesson.

"He was pretty fizzy and I couldn't make him stop," I replied, leaning down to check his girth.

"Brat!" Roisin said, fondly.

"I got off and put him away," I admitted. "Niamh said it was okay. I didn't know what was wrong."

"You know what you're doing," she replied, much to my amazement. "If it's not right, it's not right." She picked up the block and moved it away, and told me to start working him in walk.

"What if he does it again?" I asked.

"Don't worry about it," she said as she closed the arena doors. "We'll see how he goes." And for once, I didn't feel so alone, like I had to have all the answers, or a solution before anything had even happened.

Through "sharing" (for lack of a better term) with Roisin, I found a way to feel not-so-bad about stopping the ride that night. Oh, I still fought against the sincerity of the twelve-step program, much in the way I constantly questioned *how* the ladies in all the books I read bonded with their horses. It just didn't seem very "real world" to me, all the sharing and the slogans. Mind you, I could get behind "This Too Shall Pass" because I could see it work. Things did pass, things like pain and fear and sadness. As trite as I considered "One Day at a Time" to be, it certainly made it easier to manage that pain, fear, and sadness. I didn't have to get rid of those feelings I dreaded all the time, I only had to let them go for a day—for twelve hours, even. Just the daytime hours. I could do that.

Listening to people share their stories busted the myth of terminal uniqueness that plagues addicts and codependents alike. One of the reasons I loathed the Little Blue Book they distributed in Al-Anon—entitled *One Day at a Time*, in fact— because the words within perfectly expressed my experience. I didn't want to be one of *those people*, those helpless people. Up until that point, living with another's active addiction had been only *my* experience, and I got a charge out of that. But here was a book full of others (365 others, as there was a reading for each day of the year) who had similar challenges. If I wasn't the only woman suffering from this kind of havoc, then...hmmm. Then, actually, maybe I could feel less like a fool.

The Little Blue Book also told me I couldn't make an addict better through sheer force of will. So what was I doing with my life?

And if I couldn't force *myself* to be better, then where was I?

"Make," "force": harsh words. If I'd discovered nothing else from reading and Googling the phrase "horse feel," it was that gentleness tends to win the day. It goes back to "respond-ability."

Feel, in terms of working with or riding a horse, is to ask, rather than demand. And it is to know *when* to ask, *how* to ask, and how to *give*, or reward the answer you are looking for. Both on and off the horse, if you can manage to feel, but with some degree of detachment, then you are in the present moment. And that means you can respond, rather than react.

I wanted to be really good at "doing feelings"—to take responsibility for my respond-ability. In order to respond with greater flexibility, to both horses and people, there were a couple of things I had to do to change my behaviors:

1) Stop judging my insides based on other people's outsides. (This was a program-thing, obviously.) I had to stop assuming that if someone rode as if she was the poster girl for the national equestrian team, that it meant her life was perfect.
2) Don't force solutions. This was hard enough to do when I wasn't riding, so I wasn't at all sure I could do it on a horse (especially if the horse was Maverick and he came to a dead stop and I was being shouted at to make him go).
3) Keep the focus on myself. In a healthy way. Not in a pity-party kind of way.

This may have been one of my shorter lists, yet all the items seemed hard to do, the antithesis of the behaviors of a lifetime. And here repetition, as mindless as it sounded, was completely mindful. You had to repeat affirmations to get them to sink in. You had to model new behaviors to gain experience. You had to try. You had to fall. You had to get back up and go on. You had to be willing to fail. You had to *want* to succeed. In the beginning, I didn't want The Program to work. If it worked, then everything in my life at that stage, primarily the way I was behaving in my marriage, had to change.

Repetition was key to The Program: You heard the same things, over and over (and over), the same opening, the same closing. In some meetings, we passed around a sheet listing the twelve steps and everyone read one aloud (in case we missed one of the massive banners hanging on the walls, bearing, yes, all twelve steps for you to stare at for an hour).

At the end of each meeting, either holding hands or not, we said the Serenity Prayer:

> God, grant me the serenity to accept the things
> I cannot change,
> courage to change the things I can,
> and the wisdom to know the difference.

I said this in unison, with the group, week after week, day after day, meeting after meeting. I said it six days a week for several months after I made my decision to leave my marriage: twice a day when I was able to get to two meetings. I went to The Rooms and I cried; it was all I could do to sit up in a chair. What had I done? I had done something different than I had ever done in the past regarding my relationship, regarding *any* relationship I'd had: I did what I said I would do.

And when the situation did not change, I changed.

I suddenly knew the difference between what I could change and what I could not, and it just about made me sick from weeping. I wept upon waking. I wept in the evenings. At work I'd retreat to the ladies' room, some days, to cry. I cried and grieved as I gave up the urge to control.

Eventually, I began to cry only in the morning, and then again at night. And then just at night. And then I was on an every-other-day plan, and alternated crying at night with crying in the morning. It doesn't matter, I said to myself, because one day, I won't cry every day.

And one day, I didn't. That was okay, either crying or not crying; it didn't make a difference if I did or I didn't. What made the difference was that I wasn't ashamed, either by my actions, or my responses. And because I wasn't ashamed, I was able to respond to this entirely self-made situation with compassion. And because I was there, in it, and not trying to postpone it or deny it, it certainly did too pass. It was my first miracle as a result of The Program, and it was as good as winning the ribbon I still craved.

The night I pulled Maverick into the center of the arena and got off, rather than fighting on, I had the wisdom to know the difference between what had happened in that moment and in thousands of others. I responded in the moment; I could feel that he was going to take any and every opportunity to explode. I admitted to myself, and to others, that I was powerless—I could not fix it. I acted on that awareness and went up and put Maverick away.

Paradoxically, that was one of the best lessons I had that year, maybe even ever. I felt like crap all the way home, but I understood that I had made my own decision and was completely aware of how I was affecting my own experience. When I look back on that lesson, I realize *that* was when I started becoming an independent rider. I can't really describe what had felt wrong, underneath the things that were visibly wrong, between me and Maverick that night. Maybe it was the instant I began to understand what "horse feel" meant in a practical sense—that it is learned in the moment, with one horse, and then you take that to the next horse and see what works and what doesn't, and then to another, and so on. There isn't a lexicon of things to learn—of course, there are basic things you do and don't do, but you can't really map out an incontrovertible agenda because every horse is different, and you and each horse create a combination that is different from any other.

Most of all, after I got off Maverick, I didn't indulge in the catalog of reasons why I was shit. I didn't make it such a big deal. Feeling like crap "all the way home" consisted of ninety minutes. In the days of my marriage, the feeling would have lasted for days, weeks—who knows, years? But this time, I felt a feeling, allowed it to have its moment, and then it was over. I had emotions around the event, but because *I had them*, and didn't allow them to have me, I actually ended up feeling better about myself. I was proud of my decision, proud that I had kept my head, proud that I had done the right thing without caring what anybody else thought. Instead of gaining false pride from having toughed it out, I felt true pride that I was beginning to care enough about myself to make good choices.

Maybe I was beginning to love myself.

I was so delighted after I survived my very first riding lesson on Mercury, I think that might have been my first, pure, unadulterated moment of self-love. It was so unfamiliar that I have never forgotten what it felt like.

Someone else couldn't make me love myself, anymore than I could make him love me. I tried to make my husband love me, so that I would feel that I had value. Louise Hay says that all we want, any of us, in any walk of life, is love and approval.

I love you *just the way you are*—those famous three little words ought to be amended with the last five.

I harbored a feeling of deep sorrow for all the pain I knew I'd caused, from my own addiction to controlling someone else's behavior. I felt such sadness for all the rage and the resentment, for all the disappointments and the despair. I felt it all in my heart, and it felt healthy to feel it there. "True feeling is a capacity of the heart, whereas most of our emoting comes from detrimental brain patterns," I'd read somewhere. Emoting is performative, feelings are the prompts, the stage directions in the script of the stories we insist upon playing out, over and over, and the feeling itself is neither good nor bad, it just is.

For horses, emotions are just information, according to Kathy Pike. In her online essay, "How You Feel Affects Your Horse," she explains, "If a herd member becomes fearful, the whole herd responds simultaneously and moves to safety. They listen to the emotional message, take action, and then return to grazing."

In other words, horses deal with it and get over it.

"Ignoring your emotional messages takes you away from your inner wisdom," writes Pike. "These ignored emotions are held in your body and your horse responds to your whole being."

How? Apparently, the horse's heart is five times the size of that of a human being. Dr. Maria Katsamanis, a licensed clinical psychologist, certified as a mental-health professional through the Equine Assisted Growth and Learning Association, and a horse trainer, describes the workings of a horse's heart and what that can mean for us in this way:

Horses have a slower heart rate than we do. Their on/
off alarm button has been refined because of their prey
status, so that they are great role models for us to learn
how to manage our own levels of stress and alertness.

If you are having a bad day and you go into a stall
with a horse, the horse creates a "torus," a circle of
energy that embraces you. In this space, their heart
pattern, being an electrical wave, can affect our own
heart rhythms. Physically being in their space promotes
emotional and physical healing via the electro-magnetic
force created by their heart resonance.[4]

I was putting Maverick away after another night-time lesson. It hadn't been particularly trying, but it wasn't particularly
trouble-free either: it was still the same fight to get him to relax
on the bit, the same argument about exactly how fast we were
going to go, the same squabble over which lead to land on after
a jump. We rode a short course of four fences, and even though
I felt like we were fighting every stride, it was glorious fun, and I
felt like we could have jumped and jumped forever.

Back in the stable, I tucked him in. His blanket was com-
plicated, with a turtleneck-thing that flapped around his neck
and covered him up to his ears. It was in a heap in the corner of
his stall; before the lesson, he'd clearly knocked it off the door,
where it was usually folded nicely, and trampled upon it. I sighed
over that, mumbling to him, "It isn't very nice to have to wear it
after it's been lying in the muck, right? But aren't you gorgeous
in your fancy-pants blanket?"

Horse blankets are big: they cover the entire back from
withers to hindquarters, and drape down over their sides to the
tops of their legs. I heaved it over his midsection and the straps
that secure it to the horse's body went flying, the metal closures

clattering. "Probably ought to be more gentle about it," I said aloud. "But you're not going to do anything, are you, Mav? You're used to me now."

I fought a bit with the clips in the front, the ones that secured the turtleneck-thing. "These clippy bits in front are so weird!" I went on, as if he was listening. "Once I close these up, you'll be snug for sure and…"

At that stage in my monologue, I noticed that Maverick was standing still. He never stood still. He was always fussing and twitching, winnowing out leftover hay from the bedding, trying to undo the Velcro on my half chaps. But at that moment, he was not moving a muscle, and as I secured the last buckle on the front, under his throat, I realized that he had dropped his jaw to rest his head on my shoulder. I stopped chattering, so touched I thought I was going to start bawling like a baby. I rubbed my cheek against his, and I felt something coming off him, the way you can see heat coming up off the pavement in the summer. My eyes filled, and I thought to myself, Fuck's sake, conscious of the busy-ness of the main aisle of the barn as my lessonmates were settling their own mounts for the night. I breathed in, and the feeling of a wave of *something* from him intensified.

I put my arms around his neck, and whispered, "I love you."

A noise came from a stall, a shout from the aisle, and I moved away from Mav, busying myself with the straps underneath his belly. But I continued to feel everything that was going on in my heart: I was grateful for the evidence that I hadn't driven him too crazy during the past hour, that he was happy to be quiet with me, even for a minute, that he was being still enough to let me know that he knew me and that maybe he loved me, too.

I never told anyone about that night because I felt silly, but Melody Beattie came to my rescue: "Our feelings are important," she writes in *Codependent No More*. "They count. They matter. The emotional part of us is special. If we make feelings go away, if we push them away, we lose an important part of us and our lives. Feelings are our source of joy, as well as sadness, fear, and anger. The emotional part of us is the part that laughs as well as cries. The emotional part of us is the center for giving and receiving the warm glow of love."

I came to believe I had to get out of the space where I was all about emoting from my head and get in the space where I could comprehend a feeling from my heart. If I was in my heart, I had the capacity to take the good with bad, and not take it personally. I could feel things without them either taking over my life or shutting it down entirely. I could honor a time in my life and then let it go. I could grieve with intent, and know that that, too, was an act of respect: despite what occurred, and what it may have cost, the ending was a beginning, and who knew where it was going to take me?

Which was all great in theory.

When the big chestnut gelding Argo, from my second lesson ever, was at the barn one day, and gone the next, I felt prepared, a little. I hadn't ridden him in years, and yet I'd still hang out for a chat, give him a treat. He wasn't ridden in any of the lessons I was in anymore, so the separation had already begun, and there was a degree of acceptance. He was old, and he'd been retired to a pasture, which was actually really lovely because he deserved his pension.

Then, I heard one of the ladies in my Saturday lesson talking to Padraig about Argo. She was keeping him in her field, apparently. Padraig said, "It might be about that time," and my heart squeezed itself up into a little ball of pain and fear and started beating in my throat. The lady from my lesson, bless her, protested that Argo had a couple good years in him yet. But it was only a year after that when Emily asked if I missed Argo, and I began, "Oh, he's just off, enjoying his retirement..." but she started shaking her head. And I knew.

I was mounted on Cathal, and I had to turn him away from the rest of the group. I couldn't really breathe, although I knew I should, and I started to cry, quietly so that Cathal didn't freak out. Just for a few minutes, because there was a lesson to be done, and I did it, and then I let myself tear up all the way home.

I didn't pretend, either, that something wasn't bothering me over the next couple of days, because it *was* bothering me. I was sad, and when people asked me what was wrong, I told them that the first horse I'd really known was gone, and I talked about him—like the time I gave him a bit of banana, and he took it, and I thought he swallowed it, but then he opened his mouth and let it roll right out onto the ground. It was like he was saying, *bleh*! Hilarious! Oh, Argo.

I wasn't on a horse when I heard that Maverick was gone.

Maverick had a chronic injury of some sort, and it kept flaring up, so I had pretty much moved on to Cathal. He was green when he arrived at the barn, and I was playing some part in his education. It became apparent that he'd never ridden a twenty-meter circle in his life: the first one I tried in trot resulted in epic falling in. He responded to the helpfully opened inside rein by running into the outside rein and dragging us to the opposite end of the arena. Once we improved upon the trot, we moved onto canter, the first attempt of which inspired him to tank to the end of the group and keep on going—until he was tucked between the last two riders and the wall.

I regularly visited the horses I knew and didn't ride any-more, but Maverick wasn't around. Not on stall rest, then, I supposed. But after another lesson in which he hadn't appeared, I wondered to my friend Hannah what was up.

She looked at me briefly as she drove us down the long, long road, giving me a ride to the bus stop. I felt a little wave of trepidation run through me. "I heard someone say he's gone," she said, tentative.

"What?" I was stunned. I saw the world, outside the window of the car, waver for a moment. I felt like I did when I came to after having been knocked out when I fell off Ruby. I felt the pain gather and move up into my throat. I felt my eyes start to tear. I told myself to breathe, to be still, to breathe. "Gone? Like, dead?"

"No!" Hannah gasped. "I think he's for sale? I'm not sure, but he's not at the barn anymore." I could hear the sympathy in her voice. No one knows better than a horse person how attached you get. She understood. She knew how it felt. "I overheard someone say something about it tonight. I meant to see if you knew."

On the bus, I sat and stared out the window. A tear leaked out now and then; I could see my reflection—I looked devastated. I was relieved he wasn't *gone* gone, but it still felt awful. I kept it together, because I wasn't going to make a scene on public transportation—just because I was all about my feelings now didn't mean I had to have them all over the bus.

For several days, I allowed myself the time to sit still and focus on my breathing, and feel every single thing there was to feel about losing Maverick. I realized I could manage my own feelings with the same amount of gentleness and care I hoped to use in managing a horse. When I managed my feelings, good and bad, in the moment, I didn't have to control them as such, because they weren't out of control—they just were. They had the time and the space to be, and by extension, I did, too. I was at last open to living in the present.

CHAPTER SEVEN

PRESENT

I was fully feeling every emotion I had about Maverick: sadness, frustration, shock, anger. I wanted to buy him, but I didn't have the money to do so. And I shouldn't buy him because, in truth, he was not the correct horse for me. But what if I had a trainer who would work with me, who would teach me how to use all the natural horsemanship magic I read about in books, who could help get Maverick to be happy with me? What if I committed myself to making it work?

Wait—I'd been down this road before.

I almost wished I didn't know...but I couldn't pretend it wasn't happening.

I made up stories about how it all would turn out well at the end of the day—how somebody (whobody?) bought Maverick for me, and we moved him to a barn with a terrific trainer, and working together, we brought out Maverick's best, and he was happy and I was happy...and I couldn't sustain those stories, because they were not ever going to be true. The truth was, he was going to be sold, and he was going to go away, and it hurt like hell.

I couldn't do it any other way. I couldn't defer the pain. I wasn't able to live without *feeling* anymore. I'd reached the point of no return, and I didn't know what to do, except to feel all that shit. They were selling Maverick, and I didn't know how to bear it.

I bore it by feeling it, in the now.

Pain makes you focus. But what do you focus on? The pain itself? Or something else?

I couldn't talk about the end of my marriage outside a small circle of friends. I was so afraid that it would be my fault if my husband's life became shit that fear tingled up and around and through my body in great rushes. I wore my wedding ring because I was not capable of explaining why I didn't have it on. I couldn't look at the pain, I could only walk beside it, and peek at it out of the corner of my eye.

Paradoxically, however, the pain was so *there*, and I was so aware of its magnitude, that it forced me to focus on other things. This wasn't like denial, at which I was adept, where I ignored reality in order to forget about the pain. I understood that my reality was all about pain, I accepted it, and in accepting it, I figured out ways to relieve the pain as I went along. I focused on breathing, I focused on walking. I went in to work every day, and it was the best gig I ever had, because I was able to be a person designing a magazine, and I didn't have to be anything else. I listened to the same Louise Hay CD every single day for the remainder of the summer. I went to Al-Anon meetings because I knew I could talk there and no one would try to fix me. All of my energy was invested in putting one foot in front of the other and in becoming...well, not "myself" again. I had started moving toward something else.

And a large part of that movement had to do with summoning the courage to try riding a horse.

I will never, ever forget walking down that long, long road from the barn after that first lesson, after I didn't fall off, after I eventually realized that I had the power to take a tiny action that made me feel safe up there, on Mercury. I had never, ever, in all my life, felt prouder of myself than I did in that moment. I felt like every cell in my body had been shaken up in some way, energized to a degree I had never experienced before. I didn't feel like "a woman who had a failed marriage"—I felt like I was *alive*. I felt like there was hope. I felt like I could learn something new. I felt like I was more (finally) than my obsessive mind. I felt like all the pain I had endured emotionally was shifting, and though it had not been completely purged, it had at least been put to the side, somewhere neutral, for a couple of hours.

As my devotion to horses increased, the quizzical looks began. They ran the gamut from genuine curiosity, as in "that's an interesting choice of sport for an adult who has never done it before," to the slightly condescending "don't-you-have-anything-better-to-do" arched brows of those who thought "discovering" horses in midlife meant running away from something, not running toward it. I was learning new skills, I said, or I told them I was getting fit. Most people didn't want to hear that every single time I got on a horse, I had the opportunity to heal in some way. It was too "woo-woo." No one wanted to be expected to believe that an animal ("dumb," implied) was the way forward through all the shit I had managed to create for myself. Few understood that in the act of sharing breath with a horse, I was inviting an uncompromising assessment of my own being. That nothing, not one single thing that happened around and on a horse had much to do with anything outside of myself, what I was bringing to the moment, my emotional temperature, my state of physical being.

Cathal had taken to following me out of the arena at the end of a lesson without my leading him by the reins. He would stop when I stopped, and walked on when I did so. Jaws dropped and eyes lit up, and it was so gratifying for me that he had, in natural horsemanship terms, "joined up" with me, that he considered me his leader, worthy of following. And yet, as we made our way to the barn, if I started to worry he might jog off down the road, or kick out at a pony, sure enough, his pace would pick up, and I'd grab his reins before he could fulfill the rest of my nightmare scenario. Was he reading my mind? Yes, as it expressed itself through my body language, from the change in my breathing to the tensing of my muscles.

There were practical, down-to-earth lessons I learned every single hour I spent at the barn that allowed me to work with horses in a practical, down-to-earth fashion, but even getting a horse to allow me to pick up his hoof so I could remove debris prior to a ride could descend into a battle of wills in which I had the potential to come out the loser. In order for that seemingly simple task to be completed, I had to project the correct degree of assertiveness and patience, and I had to be believable in my actions. I had to squeeze the backside of the horse's lower leg in a particular place known to encourage him to raise his foot. If I just waved my hand around in the vicinity of his leg, I'd be ignored. If I squeezed, and released, and squeezed, and waited, and I didn't give up, then (eventually) we both succeeded: I communicated clearly, I did what I intended to do, and the horse got a nice clean foot.

Sometimes I would talk to someone about a horse—like the first time I rode Delilah, and how I annoyed her because I was pissed off at her for not listening to me, and how I realized I was projecting all sorts of expectations on her without clearly asking for what I wanted, and how, when I apologized to her, she put her head right over the door and leaned her chin on my shoulder. When I told a story like that, if I didn't get the curiosity or the condescension, I might get a frightened look: *She is out of her mind.*

Thank you, yes, I am out of my mind, finally, and into my body. I am feeling things through the palms of my hands, the soles of my feet, and indeed my ass, that are lifting me out of a lifetime of mental obsessing, and into a state of being that is wholly present. My attention is focused purely on the task at hand and nothing else interferes; when it does, I don't dwell on it, I correct it and return my focus to where it belongs, on the horse and what we're doing. And as I became more and more accustomed to this feeling, of being grounded in my muscles, my bones, my cells, and not "out there," somewhere in the ether of my fantasies, I started feeling more effective in my work, my relationships (of all kinds), in all aspects of my life.

I knew that endorphins—the ones I'd studied so I could explain my feelings—were the result of the physical activity related to horseback riding, and that they were producing a feeling of well-being that I had never known, or had never known to be consistent—not in a way that I could actually invoke, that was at my disposal, that wasn't a fluke or the luck of the draw. This was now a feeling I could facilitate, that I could tend to, in the sense that I could be one hundred percent *there* for it.

Could this be what all those gurus mean about "being in the present moment"?

Quite a few times I'd heard Louise Hay say the following:

> When you do not flow freely with life in the present moment, it usually means you are holding onto a past moment. It can be regret, sadness, hurt, fear or guilt blame, anger, resentment, and sometimes a desire for revenge. Each one of these states comes from a space of unforgiveness, a refusal to let go, and to come in to the present moment. Only in the present moment can you create your future.

I certainly regretted having my crop stolen. I made the mistake once of leaving it lying around the barn one afternoon, and within seconds (or so it seemed), it was gone. Pilfered. Robbed. Riding Maverick without a whip was strategically impossible, so I had to keep borrowing until I had one of my own again.

There was usually a bunch of abandoned whips lying around the place (somehow mine was never among them), but one Saturday, it didn't seem like there were any to hand. Mav and I were settling in to begin the warm-up, when I saw it.

A crop. Lying on the track in the arena, nearly buried in the sand, easy enough to miss. A mauvey-purpley affair, clearly well used, but entire, from handle to the little leather bit at the end (which probably has a proper name, but I like to refer to it as "the slappy part"). It wasn't like someone had discarded it because it was broken—it was perfectly useable. In the back of my mind, I imagined grabbing it up at the end of the lesson.

Then I forgot about it.

Or so I thought.

We jumped a cross-rail, and after a few times over, Niamh added a second fence close enough to make a "bounce," so-called because the horse couldn't take a stride between obstacles. We headed in at a trot, which Maverick didn't care for, nor was he impressed by the lowness of the fences. He jumped lackadaisically, and as we went back to wait another turn, I thought about scolding him for his laziness. Then a lessonmate, who was riding Ruby, began her approach. In the process, Ruby kicked the mauvey-purpley whip where it still lay on the ground, and I thought, No, don't break it!

That's when I realized that Maverick's attitude had everything to do with my inattention. I wasn't paying attention to our lesson or the bounce, so why should he?

By then, it was too late. Mav had clearly written me off
for the evening. Niamh added a third fence, two strides after the
bounce; we were so consistently awful at this combination that it
was astounding. I realized that I couldn't just get into the zone
after being zoned out, because the horse had a say as to whether
that mattered.

We landed after our last go, and I was so off-balance, I
almost fell off, and in trying not to fall off, I yanked on Maverick's mouth, causing him unnecessary annoyance and pain. I
wasn't good enough yet to pull myself together, and frankly, I was
so stunned to discover that I'd been obsessing about that whip
that all my focus went toward obsessing about obsessing.

Obsessing is about fear, doubt, distorted thinking, and a
basic skepticism that anything will ever work out. Whatever the
topic is, the mind takes the ball and runs with it, and runs, and
runs—and runs. This is not the least bit like riding a twenty-meter
circle over and over and over, because when you are obsessing,
you are not adjusting or correcting, or making small changes
that clarify the whole. You are only ensuring that your incorrect
thinking is building and building, in magnitude and force,
until the entire situation is mentally out of control. You may be
sitting in a chair, completely physically inactive, looking rather
still and serene, but in your head, cities are burning and tumbling
into the sea. You may be cooking dinner, looking competent and
content, and all the while you are engaging in a spot of disaster-
thinking that grows and grows until you're imagining yourself
dead on the side of the road. Linda Kohanov, author of *The Tao
of Equus*, would say your inside is not reflecting your outside, and
you are entirely incongruent. You are completely out of whack.
Your mind is going one way and your body the other.

One defining characteristic of all the self-help books I collected over time was that they all recommended *living in the present*

moment. That was where the healing and the good-life-stuff happened. But everything in my existence had been predicated upon denying that there *was* a present moment. I totally got why it was a good suggestion, not the least of which was the promise of a freedom from anxiety I wanted to experience so strongly that it made me anxious. (Why can't I live in the moment? What's wrong with me? Am I in it now? Now? *Now?*) Every move I made and every thought I had was all about minimizing past damage and preventing future destruction. I wanted The Now as much as I wanted to be a rider, because I felt like there was magic there, in The Now, and if I had that, then I could fix everything else.

I needed to get out of my mind without losing it. I had to stop being so self-conscious that I was taking myself out of the present. If I was so focused on myself and what was wrong with me and what was going to happen because of the way things had always happened in the past, I would never, ever move forward. This was my addiction. This was my drug. This was the way I dealt with the fear of the unknown, and this was how I checked out of life. I didn't need to take a pill or drink a fifth of vodka—all I had to do was let my mind go off to the races. As I began to ride, to spend time in a stable next to a horse, I began to slowly descend from the ether and get into my physical self.

It used to be so hard for me to get up in the saddle—not because of fear, but because my body didn't understand how to "get up there." I had to see myself *up there*, as I bounced and bounced on my right leg, my left foot propped in the stirrup, my left hand gripping the mane, my right hand almost entirely (Almost? Entirely!) gripping the offside bottom of the saddle as I finally summoned the nerve and hauled myself up and on.

The act of mounting was the first thing that I had to learn to do with my body and not my mind; the second thing was to sit back, when every instinct said to curl up in a ball. The third thing I learned was actually almost as tricky as learning to sit back, and that was to look where I was going. It would appear that looking where I was going would be a natural extension of paying attention, of staying in the present moment, but it was amazingly easy not to do. In a lesson on a school horse, going round and round, you could easily let the horse trot on automatic pilot and not participate in his forward movement. But when you were looking where you were going and paying attention, you were riding from your seat and influencing the way the horse was moving. Roisin would always exhort us to ride our own twenty-meter circles: look ahead to the next quarter of the circle; actively ask for the horse to flex and bend; do not merely trot along placidly, following the horse in front of you.

It was still easy enough to get caught in the habit of staring at the back of my horse's head, easy enough to get caught up in the rhythm—of the trot, especially—and just go with it. Pulitzer Prize-winning author Jane Smiley, a horsewoman, writes in her memoir *A Year at the Races* about how her position on the horse influenced not only her work in the arena, but also her presence in the world:

> I practiced keeping my heels down and my eyes up.
> The effect of this was to orient my body properly on
> the horse, and, indeed, properly on the planet, so that,
> as in walking upright, gravity would promote stability
> rather than undermine it...To look down is to enter
> into a trance of self-consciousness, and potentially, to
> fall. A rider looking down is already beginning to part
> from her horse, because her seat and thighs are already
> beginning to lift and tilt forward. Her horse is already
> beginning to react to her shift in weight by shifting his
> own weight. He is getting ready to stumble.[5]

I'm fairly certain I've spent most of my life walking with my gaze glued to the pavement. When I lived in New York City, I was pathologically obsessed with picking up pennies, mainly because I always saw the stupid things. And I always saw them because I was always, always looking down. I was walking up Seventh Avenue once, saw a penny, picked it up, and some dude passing on my right smiled at me and said, "Good luck!"

I replied, "I think I should be looking up at the sky, or something, you know?"

He laughed, and we went our separate ways.

In Ireland, that's where I began to see everything: On the north side of Dublin, walking past Connolly Station, I saw the people swarming out of the station itself, I saw the crowd surging against the light to cross to Talbot Street, I saw the taxis pulling out of the rank, I saw the buses trundling back up the coast road, and in the distance, I saw one of the trams from the Luas line, the light rail system that runs in city center, curving away toward Abbey Street. I saw it all, because my head was up, my eyes were forward, and my chin was down.

One of my lessonmates once said that she'd started to drive a car like she was riding, meaning she was very, very aware of both sides of her body at the same time. I'd started to correct my walk the way I would correct myself in the saddle. I would catch myself leaning forward, and I'd consciously sink back into my hips, tuck the back of my neck into my collar, drop my chin. I would swiftly catch myself spacing out, gazing into the gutter, and pick up my head.

A forward gaze is confident, assured, and the rest of the body follows, up and out and forward. Is it mind over matter, or matter over mind? I think it's actually about healing this dualistic split, about making the self whole. It's not either/or, it's both/ and. Sometimes I need to think with my head, but I also need to allow my body to speak its own mind—and, sometimes, to make decisions for me.

Early in my riding career, I started my week off with a lesson on Monday morning. There was nothing better than starting the week with a lesson under my belt—and nothing worse than having to get out of bed at 5:50 a.m. to get to the barn in time.

Anytime the alarm went off at stupid o'clock and I had to get up, even if it was for something that I loved to do, my first impulse was to stay curled up under the covers. If it seemed like it might be raining the first time the buzzer buzzed, that was reason enough to blow the lesson off. Somewhere between the second and third time I hit snooze (I hate mornings) I would somehow find myself on my feet, and by the time I remembered to kill the fourth alarm, I'd have gotten myself into my gear and out the door. I'd be on my bus, wondering how I'd gotten there.

My body got me out the door. As "heady" as I have always been my whole entire life, my body seemed to have finally found its voice, and its authority: One minute I'd be dreaming away the morning, and the next I'd be fully clothed, standing at the bus stop.

If my body could speak, I expect its Monday-morning pep talk would have sounded something like this:

> Nope, let's go! Come on! It's not raining, it might not
> rain, even if it does rain by the time you get on the
> long road, there are plenty of trees, you won't get too
> wet, you won't get soaked, come on: Jodhs on! Top—
> on! Bag packed, zip up the half chaps, don't mind the
> coffee, you'll survive, put on the fleece, the next jacket,
> the big jacket, sling the bag on your shoulder, keys,
> open the door, lock the door, go, go, go!

And by the time I got to the barn, there was nowhere else I'd rather be.

○

Even after a couple of years of horseback riding, and the presence of real evidence that Al-Anon worked—mainly, that I had truly left my marriage—I continued to react to its teachings with cynicism. Everyone was so grateful all the time, talking about the Gifts Of The Program, that I sometimes just ran in, sat through the meeting, and ran right back out so I wouldn't have to hear that kind of stuff. Whenever other attendees talked about the gift of doing service—acting as secretary for the group, as treasurer, as the maker of tea—well, if I rolled my eyes with any more energy, they would have spun 360 degrees in my skull.

There was one meeting, though, where no one did any service at all. It was a drag not to have a cup of tea, but since this was acquired behavior on my part, and not embedded in my DNA as it was for the Irish members, I wasn't really bothered. However, no one was acting as secretary, the individual responsible for reading the opening and closing, and asking people to share, and it was annoying. I mean, you showed up for a meeting and expected a meeting to happen, right? I *needed* that meeting—it suited me time-wise and location-wise, and why didn't somebody step up?

Well, someone suggested I step up. Uh, hello? We weren't supposed to be telling each other what to do, right? I'd only been in The Program a little while. Why weren't there any veterans around to handle it? I felt like all my life I was always filling in because no one else would show up, and I was sick of it. Part of my recovery was to say no when there was someone else perfectly able to do whatever needed doing, wasn't it?

Frankly, I was scared to death. There was no way I wanted to be sitting up there—*me*, bossy old me, always getting into trouble organizing and managing things because people ended up being resentful. Why should I stick my neck out? What if I did it and I did something wrong? What if no one showed up? What if no one would speak? What if someone did speak...on and on and on? How was I supposed to control a group of people with problems with control? Besides, bad things happened when I was in charge of them.

There was no way I was going to agree to be secretary.

I agreed to be secretary.

It was only for three months—the exact amount of time I thought I needed to be done with the whole Al-Anon business altogether. I sat at a table at the front of the room, my heart beating in my throat. I kept paging through the binder, checking my lines, reading the opening and closing bits over and over, consulting the cheat sheet another equally nervous member had cribbed on a scrap of paper and left behind. (A list! Hallelujah!)

It occurred to me that I had to ask someone to speak, and I did, and she said no, and I smiled and thanked her and moved on.

Holy shit, I thought. That person said no, and I smiled and said thanks and moved on.

I didn't get angry or sad or rejected. I asked someone else. That person said yes.

They joined me at the table, and I didn't feel so frightened and alone at the front of the group. But we just sat there, next to each other. We didn't chat, as the person was concentrating on choosing a page to read from The Little Blue Book, and I kept checking my lines. No need to check my pulse; it had moved from my throat to hammer in my ears.

People drifted in, some sat alone, some chatted with each other. The clock on the wall crept to zero hour (I had arrived twenty-five minutes early and felt like I had been there for about a week), and I looked up, said hello, introduced myself, said I'd open the meeting, and I did.

About halfway through, after the main speaker had read her bit and spoke, after I threw the meeting open to anyone who wanted to share, I realized that my heart rate had quieted, evened out. I wasn't worried anymore. I breathed and I felt an incontrovertible and utterly tangible wave of serenity begin to flow through my entire body. I didn't have to do anything. I didn't have to work too hard. I just had to sit there and let the meeting happen. I just had to trust that it was going to take care of itself. I could only do my part, my fifty percent, and the group had to do theirs.

This was not my expectation. I thought that I would have to be in charge. I didn't want to be in charge. I had been in charge of the marriage and look how that worked out. I expected the meeting to go the same way, but somehow, it didn't.

The Program, in fact, suggested that I *not* have expectations. This, in turn, drove me round the bend. How could I *not* have expectations? Wasn't *not* having expectations what got me into my marriage mess in the first place? Wasn't my self-esteem so low as to preclude high expectations? I knew that deep down, in my heart of hearts, I did not expect my partner to pay his bills, or to change and suddenly wake up one day, having embraced recovery. Since I did not expect that to happen, I ran around trying to make sure that at least the status quo was maintained, by me, entirely on my own.

Having Al-Anon tell me not to expect anything was infuriating! How was my life supposed to improve, how was my relationship—all my relationships—supposed to get better if I didn't *expect* them to get better?

When I started riding horses, the only expectation I had was that I would learn how not to fall off. I expected to learn how to avoid breaking any of my bones. My heart was already broken; I didn't have it in me to deal with anything else. It sounded melodramatic to describe it that way, but whenever I thought about the situation (Should I find a lawyer? Would my ex ever pay back the money he owed me? Did he have a job? Was he okay? Was he *alive*?) I felt a physical pain in my chest. I found, though, that I didn't think about any of that, any of those worries, when I was at the barn. And all I thought about when I was up on a horse was staying up there.

I experimented with the "whispery stuff"—the natural horsemanship the ladies in the horse books wrote about. If I got to the barn early, I would stand outside Argo's stall, if he wasn't in a lesson, and chatter away to him, and try to get him to let me touch his cheek. I wouldn't reach out so much as just put my hand up and see if he chose to make the connection. I didn't try to make him do it; I simply created the space for him to do it if he wanted. Maybe he would rest his cheek in my palm for a moment. The day he did, it was a major victory. I had always striven so hard to do things, that this—so small, so gentle—was a crowning achievement. I had taken knowledge I had only read about in a book and made it concrete in the world. I hadn't expected it to work, and I suppose that's why it did. I "got out of the way," as Louise Hay would say, and let it happen.

In that moment, even though I still had a lot to learn, it seemed it was maybe, actually learnable. I knew for sure now there was more to this riding gig than just preventing a fall.

"Has anybody ever jumped before?"

It was the middle of December. I had been riding for... thirteen weeks. Twice a week since the middle of November, so that was more like sixteen weeks if you counted the other days as weeks, as one lesson per week, and...

...I was still bouncing around trying to stay on the correct diagonal—when I was supposed to rise in the saddle at the trot—and feeling pretty lucky Argo spoke English, because while my leg aids for the canter were still unintelligible to him, he got there if Niamh told him, "Can-TER! Can-TER!" So, still a beginner, then. Gaining in confidence, ready for more, sure—but jumping? Wasn't that how people broke their necks? Niamh set a series of poles flat on the ground, and everyone in my lesson looked at each other, grimacing dubiously.

We learned jumping position. We trotted over the poles (God only knew why) with our bums in the air, hands clutching manes. We'd all just about managed to figure out how to sit properly in the saddle (just) and now we had to hover over it—while the horse leaped over a fence.

What?

We lined up at M, preparatory to taking turns over the fence. And when I say "fence," I mean two poles crossed between uprights about, oh, six inches off the ground.

I went first.

Argo pranced in place, ears perked. Seemed like somebody was looking forward to this. Thank God one of us knew what we were doing. Kicking him into trot, I reverted to the hundred-mile stare into the back of his head, as if it were a door to be unlocked, or a screen upon which all the knowledge I didn't possess would display itself.

"Look at your jump!" shouted Niamh.

Argo swung around the corner. I was rising in the trot, and Niamh shouted to kick him on. I was rising and trotting and kicking and rising and there was the fence, and the pole on the ground in front of the fence, and we got to the pole and I lifted my bottom like I was supposed to and suddenly there was this feeling, a feeling of collection, a lift, a little skip, and we were up and over, and I thudded back down into the saddle.

"Well done!" Niamh shouted, and I looked up at the other riders, and they were all beaming at me. I clapped Argo on the shoulder, on the base of his neck, with my still trembly hand, and he shook his head like, *Yeah!*

And I wanted to go again and again and again.

I had no expectations regarding jumping. I didn't expect to jump that day, or to jump *ever*, but there I was. Expectations are all about the future and often are based on hope that something is going to be different, be better than it is now. My marital expectations were like that, but as Louise Hay told me repeatedly, you can't create the future from the garbage of the past.

I eventually stopped reckoning how many weeks it had been since I started riding. It was like the counting, the adding up, was a way to tell myself how I was doing, that it somehow became a symbol of my worth. If time accumulated, then so would my value. I counted the weeks until I got to eighteen. It was somewhere around year three that I realized that time didn't matter anymore. Every single hour in the saddle was completely different. The best I could do was the best I could do, and I did my best to manage the variables, because there were always variables. What were the weather conditions? Was it rainy, was it blowy? How was my health? Did I have a cold coming on? Had I been out too late the night before? Was my horse tired? Bored? Some instructors may think they can shout you better, but everything has to be taken into consideration, put into perspective, and weighed. Eventually, a rider understands she is only fifty percent of the equation. She understands she will be forever and always learning.

I slowly began to acknowledge that I could only ever do my own fifty percent in *any* relationship. That included my relationship to a higher power. I was trying too hard to figure God out, and when I was trying too hard to figure something out, odds were I was only using my intellect. I decided to stop trying to figure out the "higher power thing." I kept up with the readings in The Little Blue Book, but I stopped expecting to find definitive answers. I could read and read and read, but until I actually took what I needed off the page and incorporated it into my life, it was all meaningless.

Incorporate, from the Latin: to form into a body. Until I began to truly inhabit my body, with all its strengths and weaknesses and cellulite, I was only fifty percent engaged with my life. I read all those books about horses and recovery, but until I put the information into action—physically and emotionally—it was only words. By checking myself when I began dissociating, and feeling whatever feelings needed to be felt, I anchored myself in reality. By embodying all I learned in my lessons and in The Rooms, I was better able to become what I wanted to be: strong, teachable, joyful, flexible, assertive, compassionate. The more I was all those things, the more I liked being where I was, which was Here. The more I was *Here*, the more I was in the *Now*. The more in the Now I was, the less I worried. The less I worried, the freer I was. The freer I was, the better I lived.

The freer I was, the better I rode.

I didn't know I was having one of my last rides on Maverick. He was fizzy, but it was a manageable kind of fizz. The belly-button thing was working like a charm on twenty-meter circles: Every time I felt him start to fall in I shifted in the saddle and pointed my navel at his inside ear. After a stride or two, he'd prevent himself from tipping over, I'd nudge him with my inside leg, and he paid attention to the correction. Later in the lesson, he was literally lunging at fences, taking off from waaay out, making it tricky for us to get the correct distance for the second fence of the combination—but for whatever reason, it wasn't a big deal. I also got to practice that thing with my butt again, the pinching thing that made him shorten up his stride. It made me laugh, the way it worked, how tensing up my ass made everything change on horseback.

"That was crazy," I said to Hannah, as she drove me to the bus stop afterward. "Crazy, but in a reasonable way."

"I don't know how you trust him," Hannah replied with a shudder. "I trust Felix, but I don't know...is that a mistake? Am I taking it for granted that he'll behave?"

"Maybe," I said, thinking about the tidy gray gelding she preferred to ride. "Or, because you trust him, you're relaxed, and he feels your relaxation, and then he relaxes, and the whole situation just feeds on itself, in a good way."

Maybe Mav and I had more trust than I thought. Whenever we jumped a series of fences, as we had that night, we had so much to do, and I had so much to think about, I mostly just left him to it and focused on getting us around the place. I trusted that once Maverick had seen a fence, he was going to go over it. He wouldn't put in a dirty stop, I knew that much. Since I trusted him to jump, the fact that he was taking off really early... well, I just went with it.

He needed to be able to trust me to do my job, too, which was to notice that, hey, he was taking off really early and not getting the distance right, so therefore perhaps I should pinch up my butt. When we tried the combination of fences again, it was perfect.

So maybe Maverick trusted me to pay attention and make necessary adjustments?

I don't know that I *trusted* Maverick in the pure sense of the word. I knew I could *rely* on him...to be stroppy, frustrating, and moody. "Rely" could mean many things, like "count on," which seemed to work in the context of Maverick...in a less than positive sense. I suppose the answer was to be able to rely on myself, to know that I would be present, in the moment, in every moment that made up my riding lesson, and that I would flex as necessary.

Whenever someone got into trouble in a lesson, Niamh always gently called out, "Use your riding!" meaning, use the stuff we already knew that worked. The first few times she sent that advice in my direction, I didn't know what she was talking about it. But I would eventually get it. Sitting back worked. Lowering my hands worked. Waiting for the horse to take the fence worked (rather than throwing myself forward in the saddle, as had been my wont). It was about bringing my useful past experiences into the Now moment. I was finally in the place where I understood (acknowledged, knew, was aware, was conscious of the fact) that I had to *be there*, every single second I was in the saddle. There was even more Now to be experienced.

It was very exciting.

"Working The Program" meant applying the principles of twelve-step to your daily life. It was all well and good to sit in a room for an hour and be on track and in control in a meeting, but the whole point was to be able to behave in the same healthy, compassionate, noncontrolling ways in the real world. The Little Blue Book didn't say this in so many words, of course, because Al-Anon liked to keep things simple. That's why the steps were almost terse in their brevity, why all the slogans were no more than four or five words. You didn't need a lot of words to express the ideas.

I like words, and the more words the better. That's why The Speech developed, because I thought, Hey, if I just keep talking, I will talk this situation into little bits and pieces, and it will eventually change. One of the reasons I hated The Program was that everything was so short and to the point. You'd be going on and on, exposing your soul to another member, and at the end of it, she'd say, "One day at a time!" It drove me completely mental, enraged me, because...because it scared me to death. Communication of The Program ideas was straightforward, no waffling, no excuses. I sneered at the sincerity because I found it threatening. Genuine feelings expressed without an attempt at manipulation? I hadn't the first notion what that meant.

I fought The Program at first because, although I didn't know it at the time, I was worn out from fighting the disease, and I had to have something to fight. To begin with, getting me to subscribe to the notion that addiction was a disease took me ages. It felt like a cop out, a justification, more mollycoddling of a thing that was so insidious, so foul, so destructive, that to give it the label of "disease" seemed to take it off the hook. I did not believe that there was a cure; I believed that addictions remained unmanageable forever. I also believed that the minute you let down your guard, you would be defeated.

I took addiction on, every day. Sometimes, my only thought upon waking was, I am going to beat this today. I am going to take care of business; I am going to make everything work; I am going to win, win, win. I am going to succeed where no one has before. I am going to write a book about The Things to Do to Make Someone Stop Misusing Substances. To hell with that disease bullshit. He is making choices, so I am just going to have to help him make other choices.

That was another part of the thin edge of my recovery wedge, but I needed to make an adjustment, to say: *I am going to make other choices.* The things that I thought were expectations were actually values; I had to change that perception. I could choose to pay all the money for the New Place and the New Start (again), or I could choose not to. I could choose to leave. I could choose to go to meetings and use the steps and slogans. I could choose to do service. I could choose to allow The Program to do what it says it will do: give me the space to find the courage to change.

Eventually, every single thing that I saw as a weakness in myself was, in fact, a strength. Every single thing that made no sense to me about The Program and that I thought could never, ever work became the only sensible way to move forward, the only way to clear out the muck I'd accumulated.

The Program had no expectations of me. Therefore, I was liberated.

I had to begin to act in ways that seemed to me to be counterintuitive:

1) I had to stop trying to fix things.
2) I had to mind my own business.
3) I had to stop looking outside of myself for someone to save, so he, in turn, would be able to save me.
4) I had to look at *my own* contribution to every single event and situation in my life—the bad as well as the good.

I had to do all that...and then let it all go. *Surrender* was the only way forward. I had to stop working so hard, had to give up on the idea of that blue ribbon, because it was a reward for being a martyr, and frankly, I studied art history, and I'd seen what happened to the likes of Saints Stephen and Lucy. I didn't need to go to such dramatic lengths to prove to the world that there was a god or gods in my life. It began to be apparent that as long as I was in the present moment, then I was in the presence of my own power, and acknowledging my own power was as good as having a higher power any day.

I was given that gift every time I got up on a horse. When people continued to ask me, "Why horses?" I said, "Because they have been my only experience of the present moment." Horses allowed me to take all the stuff I learned in all the self-helping, spiritual books I read and put their tools into practice. They showed me that I was teachable. I could learn something new. I could release the expectation that everything was always going to turn out the way it had in the past, for I now had the ability to let go and allow the next moment to unfold. I could create space for new experiences and not let past (bad) experiences interfere.

I had fallen off the big gray horse and broken my bottom on that first ride in the spring of 2003. By June of 2007, even after ten months of lessons, I was still scared stupid of riding outside the fenced or covered arenas. So, one Tuesday, when Niamh said we were going to ride into the fields, I could feel the old fear tingling along my nerve endings. I could still see that picture in my head: the guide and my friend in front of me, ready to continue ambling down the wooded path. I could see the puddle; I could feel my entire body dissociating, cell by cell...I could feel my body hitting the ground.

On top of that, I was slightly peeved to be given Argo, my beloved Argo, always beloved! But, well, I'd moved on. I was better than Argo! Grumpy, slow, old Argo, with his ponderous trot and his increasingly stiff canter.

Then I got it—he wasn't going to go crazy, leaping and bucking all over the place. At least I was pretty sure he wouldn't. I reckoned it was unlikely that he was going to go haring off toward the horizon, but on the other hand, he had been known to get seriously annoyed by the exuberance of others, and there was plenty of exuberance around: the ponies ready to go mad with the freedom of being out of the ring, the turned-out horses calling to each other, rolling around on the ground. He could react by trying to get away from them...he could start galloping, out of control...

My group walked out of the indoor arena and headed past the parking lot; Argo and I were buried in the middle. He cantankerously picked his way around the parked cars, my foot swinging dangerously close to a sideview mirror. He pricked his ears up as we angled away from the road that lead to the outdoor arena, and we headed toward the driveway. He sighed heavily.

I made sure that I had plenty of contact everywhere it was possible to have contact. The road was deserted—teatime, Tuesday night—and we walked down the lane and trotted back up without incident. Argo was sluggish. No one got hurt. We meandered back through the parking area, past the indoor arena, past the barn, up a slope to a gate.

I lifted my gaze to the top of the hill that lay past that gate, up at the sky that was still so blue, as blue as midday, even though it was after 7:00 p.m. A breeze came up from miles away, off Dublin Bay, and a horse in a nearby run-in whickered contentedly. I had to agree: it was a beautiful night.

"Right," called out Niamh from the front of our meandering line. "We're going to canter up this hill. Shorten your reins, lean forward in a light seat, not quite jumping position but—"

But I didn't hear any more. Canter? Up that hill? The high one? What?

We walked up to the gate.

"Light seat? Which leg?" I muttered to myself, to Argo—and suddenly the first horses in the group went flying up the hill, and Argo channeled some fire from his younger days, and we followed. My body naturally folded forward, I lifted my bottom, I dropped my heels, I clutched Argo's sides with my calves—and okay, I cheated and grabbed some mane, too—and then I hollered, whooped, laughed like a loon as we flew forward, up, up, up the green, green hill to the highest point of the most beautiful field in the world at a million miles an hour under the bluest summer sky.

I had felt so sad about Maverick leaving—but I really felt it. I felt everything I had to feel, I didn't shove anything to the side, I didn't deny or project or obsess. Which is just as well, as I would have been wasting my energy: He had an owner who had been lending him to the riding school, and due to Mav's recurring injuries, made the best decision for him and took him off work. I was fantasizing and daydreaming (again!) about an unavailable being. I was reacting to incomplete information, and while I had every right to feel loss and move through it, there were missing pieces to the story, things I didn't know.

What do I know for sure? I know that horseback-riding requires my entire being—mind, body, and spirit. That life is really easy when I keep the focus on myself without becoming overly self-conscious. That not only am I learning to do a new activity, I am also learning more and more about myself every day. When I realized that the crazy shit I was trying to control was a reactionary way to manage my fear, and my fear of feelings, it was then I started to live in the present, and built a strong, healthy life for myself. The road to recovery, which I'd resisted and had seemed murky, had become clear.

CHAPTER EIGHT

CLEAR

I had picked up an injury: I didn't break a bone, but tore a muscle in my left lower leg, on the inside, in between the muscle-y part of my calf and my ankle. I had been practicing for a dressage test at the barn I went to on Mondays, and I couldn't get Joxer to stay in the area defined by the white plastic boundary markers laid out on the ground. I think I must have simultaneously dropped my heel and kicked—once the adrenaline and endorphins had left my bloodstream, I realized, hmmm, something feels funny.

My physiotherapist told me I'd most likely be unable to ride for two to four weeks.

I sat at home, on the couch, sending all my mental energy to that torn muscle. I applied cold packs, I rubbed arnica cream on the area, I took arnica tablets three times a day. I got healing magnets and became a connoisseur of medical tape. I breathed and breathed, and the day I got back up in the saddle and started to trot, well, it was the best day of my life. I had made it back in two weeks.

Two weeks after my return to riding, I jumped up, celebrating a scored goal in the World Cup (USA vs. Slovenia), and found myself on the floor. I couldn't walk home from the pub—it felt like my entire foot was frozen. I had re-torn the muscle and also jammed my Achilles, which had been a weak point in my physicality since the mid-nineties. I couldn't believe the pain...and a new fear blossomed: would I ever ride again? A bit melodramatic? Maybe, but going from four lessons a week to barely being able to walk a hundred yards scared the crap out of me.

I went to my physiotherapist every two weeks, took arnica any way I could get it, massaged the area, cold-packed it morning, noon, and night. I bought those support-sock things, and discovered that FitFlops™ were the only shoes I could walk in. Two more weeks went by, and I thought I was going to go crazy. So I went back to the barn...and Delilah. She understood that something was up and took care of me, behaved impeccably, listened to me at every turn—she didn't even bite me once the entire time. Since horseback riding required I put weight into my heels, I stretched the notoriously hard-to-reach Achilles tendon, and I slowly improved.

Then the lesson times and instructors' schedules got shifted around for the autumn, and I ended up in the Saturday midday lesson.

This was an experienced crowd who had been riding together for years. I was at the back of the group again. I felt defensive about not being able to ride at their level because of the fucking injury. When I explained what had happened, I felt like I was just making excuses.

In my first lesson, despite knowing better, I tried to take a fence on Delilah, and fell on my head. Literally.

Then, one Saturday, I was told to ride Cathal.

When I got on Cathal, he balked.

I asked again, more firmly, for him to walk on, and he shook his big butt.

Oh, no you don't, I thought.

"Oh, no you don't," I said, "Dude," and his near ear twitched back toward me. "I have been riding Maverick for the guts of four years. You, young sir, are an amateur." I gave him a twitch to the rump with my short stick, which I backed up with a firm leg, and he walked on.

It took several steps before I adapted to the rolling quality of his gait. We bumped and grinded down to the lower arena... where he balked some more.

I thought to myself, I need a long stick.

So I called out: "I need a long stick," and someone swapped crops with me.

As the lesson went on, I made a list in my mind of Cathal's strengths and weaknesses, of the things he did (like holding his head kind of high: was it me and my bad hands, or his habit?) and things he didn't do (lead with the proper leg going to the right, in canter). I asked questions of him, got answers, and rode him with my mind and my body.

I made decisions for myself without anyone saying, "You should use a long stick with him." I came to my own conclusions, for the first time ever.

For the first time ever, I got on a horse and figured out what to do.

Very early on, within the first six months of riding, I would stand next to whichever horse I'd been assigned, waiting for the instructor to come along and chivvy me up into the saddle. There was a girl working at the barn—from Austria, maybe—and she *totally* knew what she was doing. I would watch her as she went around the horse, authoritatively yanking down stirrups, checking the girth, making adjustments without even thinking.

The day I found myself doing all that stuff, all that "equestrian stuff," all by myself, was a big day. Any day I made a decision for myself on or around a horse was a big day. Any day that

I made a good, informed decision that had long-term impact on my well-being in *any* area of my life was a good day, a day that proved that I was capable of clarity: of transparency, no longer obfuscating to make life easier in the short term, no lying, no fudging, none of those maladaptive codependent behaviors. I could see a situation clearly, and I could be clear about my responses. Clarity is also the quality of being coherent. Coherence meant I was becoming whole, consistent, and by extension, trustworthy to myself. I was beginning to stockpile good outcomes.

If the brain is a repository of bad outcomes, it stands to reason that it also contains good ones. Those bad outcomes eventually become information with no emotional charge, information you can use to create a different outcome, a better one, if you keep applying yourself with help and patience.

For some reason, for an entire term, none of us in the Tuesday lesson could look where we were going when approaching an obstacle. It was comical because where were we looking if not where we were going? Yet our instructor's patience never faltered.

Then it all clicked; she had us jump fences that had funky approaches so we would *have to* look where we were going or else end up a mess. The simplicity of the movement was powerful: the act of the rider turning her head turns her spine, which shifts her seat, so the horse gets the message, Go *that* way. We learned we *would* get to the fence, even though it looked like there was no way we were going to have the space or the time. Looking where you are going? Duh. Listening to instructions? Bigger duh. Once we got it, once it became clear that it worked, we had rewired our brains and created muscle memory—and then we moved on to the next thing we needed to correct.

In the spirit of this, I decided the folks who developed The Program probably knew what they were doing, and I may as well go along with it. In The Rooms, I became accustomed to speaking my truth, and no one told me I was wrong. Something similar had happened to them, and they believed me, without reservation.

No one said I was hysterical because I was afraid of losing my home and ending up in the street, that I was afraid my partner would end up in jail because of the stealing and the violence—that I was afraid the violence was going to find its way home.

No one told me to stay or go because the power of The Program was in learning my own mind, saying what I thought, getting used to the sound of my own voice telling the truth, and of the strength gained from making decisions in my own favor, at last.

I didn't talk to non-members about The Program, and I stopped talking about my situation altogether outside The Rooms due to others projecting their fears (of abandonment, of their own involvements with addiction) onto me, and of their judgments about how I should have tried harder, should have been more compassionate—what was wrong with me, that I made him act like that? I said nothing until someone asked me how I managed, what was I doing to be feeling so well, considering my marriage had ended? And then God help me (and them, too, maybe) I shared.

I read The Little Blue Book every day looking for resonance within myself from the stories others told. I had done The Fourth Step: "Made a searching and fearless moral inventory of ourselves." I catalogued my defects of character and worked on trying to find the gold in the dross. I kept the focus on myself. I stopped forcing solutions.

I did my best not to get myself into a panic when I moved from the bedsit to a gorgeous one-bedroom apartment that looked out over Dublin Bay. I felt myself obsessively worrying about the actual, physical move. I struggled not to mentally collect all the bits and pieces of my life I had strewn all over town—storage space west of the city center, the basement of the office building where I worked, the bedsit itself—over and over and over, like I was planning the siege of Rome. I told myself that it would all get done, one step at a time, one minute at a time, one box at a time, and so it did.

I managed to control my desire to unpack everything all at once, to get it all over with. I managed not to melt down when I unpacked boxes that had held actual physical objects—the duvet from the bed, the fancy pots and pans—we had shared. I called a member, talked about what I was feeling. It made me feel better. I had The Program, and I wasn't afraid to use it.

The barn periodically held jump shows, known as The League, on Sundays throughout the year. These were low-stress affairs meant to provide a little healthy competition, to test what we'd been learning. The Spring League of 2012 had been going on for ages, and in no time at all there was only one more show left. I had talked myself out of it the first week, and after that, there wasn't even a voice in my head to ignore. I was doing okay on Cathal, but every fence felt like a fifty-fifty proposition, and I wasn't feeling sufficiently confident. Then the Saturday before the very last competition, one of the ladies in my lesson talked me and Amy, one of my riding pals, into going.

I was unexpectedly out that night, home at midnight(ish), and when I woke up on Sunday, I thought, Ah, no, I'll sleep in and forget it.... But as usual, I found myself up, washing my face, having coffee, checking the bus times, and walking out the door with horses on my mind.

At some stage on the bus, it occurred to me that just because I'd been riding Cathal of late didn't mean I had to jump him that day. I thought, Maybe I'll take Delilah? I knew she wasn't terribly supple and was getting up in years, but I'd watched her jump a number of fences for a very indifferent rider fairly recently, and she cleared them all.

Cathal or Delilah? Delilah or Cathal? went my brain, getting me back for ignoring its plea to have a lie-in instead of a show-jump.

Amy's car was waiting for me at the bus stop. I got in and barely said hello, just: "I might take Delilah."

"Oh, yeah?" Amy pulled away from the curb and headed for the main road. "Her canter's pretty sticky."

"I saw her jumping in a lesson the other week and she went clean over everything."

Amy looked dubious. "She always puts in that half-stride before a fence."

"But if I'm aware of it, I can do something about it." I glanced out the window. The weather looked good, one less thing to worry about. "I jumped her over a course once, that time, like, four years ago. We didn't go clear." That hadn't been her fault. But still..."Maybe Cathal's better."

"You've been riding him a while," Amy replied, content to debate the topic. "It makes sense."

"He's got that stop in him, though. He might be better in the arena, by himself?" I wondered, and on we went, weighing the pros and cons of the two horses between us.

Ah, pros and cons. They always make for a good list. Always excellent fodder for endless mental obsessing. If I did this instead of that, the other would occur. Or would it? Maybe I ought to do that, instead of this, and then—but no, the other really was contingent on this, not that, right?

Sometimes, it actually produced anxiety to *not* have my mind going around in circles.

And sometimes, my anxiety forced me to "get stuff off my chest," and so I shared in meetings, even when I didn't want to. I talked from my head, and because I do things according to the rules, I always structured my talking in tandem with the theme of the meeting—be it the reading of the day's page from The Little Blue Book, or The Step of the Day, or this or that slogan. I listened to myself talk, delighted that I sounded so thoughtful. I prepared my statements while other people took their turns, pretty sure that what I was going to say would be smart and probably help someone else in the room.

As I went to more meetings, and began to let The Program work, I slowly stopped *listening* to myself talk and began to *hear* my *self* speak. When my *self* spoke in meetings, saying what I didn't feel I could say anywhere else, telling the truth felt pretty scary. There were no lies when my *self* spoke. At first, it would speak, and I'd tell it, Fuck off, self, who asked you? But because no one else spoke directly to me or responded with an opinion to what I said, all I could do was hear my *self*, and eventually it wouldn't fuck off anywhere when I told it to.

The day I actually began to speak rather than talk, the day that I said fuck it to the reading or the step or the whatever, the day that I actually said what was in my heart, was the day that I realized that nobody could actually tell me anything.

It was about a month after my separation was officially official, after I had gotten everything that I could manage out of the house that we'd shared, after I'd written all the letters to close joint accounts, after I'd gotten him to sign stuff. I met him at a café, and we dealt with the keys to the storage space, I drank tea that didn't taste like anything, and he started going on about how "if only he'd done things differently twenty years ago" and I whispered into the tea cup, "I never have to listen to anything like this ever again." I got up, and walked out, and he sat there, and all I knew was that it was vital that I keep walking, walking to the corner, around the corner, to the bus stop, onto the bus, to my own place, where I could close the door and lie down and breathe. Every single step broke my heart. Every single step straightened my spine. I began to understand that I could be both sad and strong.

I perceived light at the end of the tunnel. I knew that I was going to be okay.

I knew that, and nobody had to tell me. I knew it because I could hear, underneath the tears and the pain, my sheer, bone-stubborn determination to heal and live. I totally and completely gave up trying to fight any of that shit, anymore. Addiction was so much bigger than me, and it was nothing I could control, ever, so I was going to just get control of myself. After all, I had my own addiction, trying to make sure that everyone else was happy so that I could be happy. I was going to quit trying to fix that, too. What would it be like to devote all the time and energy I had previously devoted to my marriage to healing myself? I thought that might be like getting better.

Actually, I knew that's what it was, and nope, I didn't need anyone else to tell me it was what I should do.

I didn't really need Amy to tell me whether to ride Cathal or Delilah that Sunday in The League, but it was worth it to me to hear myself try to figure it out. The thing about riding Cathal was this: I had started riding him when I was less than 100 percent healed from my calf injury, and while I was trying to learn his idiosyncrasies, and use my riding skills, I wasn't as strong as I needed to be, and I had fallen off him. A lot. Like, every Saturday for a year. It was infuriating, embarrassing, and occasionally it was painful. But the fact was that he was being absolutely correct: I was supposed to be giving him the proper aids that would tell him what I wanted him to do, and if he didn't get those aids from me, he wouldn't know what to do. Or if I was nervous jumping, and tugged on the reins, his cue to stop, as we were heading toward a fence, he'd either lose confidence in me, or do what the aid told him to do and stop.

And off I'd go.

I'd fall because I didn't have the strength to grip with my left leg, and I was too afraid to try to grip because I didn't want to tear the muscle all over again.

I started dreading Saturdays, which was upsetting because my very first riding lesson had been on a Saturday, and that was special to me. I stuck with it, though, and one Saturday as my lessonmates and I left the arena, I announced, with a little bit of surprise, "Hey! I didn't fall off!" And then, the next month I said, "Hey! I haven't fallen off in five Saturdays!" And then one day, I was going to fall off Cathal—he ran out on the second fence of three-in-a-row, a "triple combination," at the last possible minute, and I felt myself begin to slide, and I simply reached out, grabbed the jump standard, gripped with my outside leg, which was luckily my right one, and slid myself back into the saddle, while I cried out, "I am NOT falling off this fucking horse!" And I didn't. Everyone in my lesson went, "Wooooooo!" and I felt as good as if I had jumped the fence itself.

But falling off that fucking horse was still a distinct possibility, which was why I was hemming and hawing about riding Delilah instead. Which seemed a little crazy because I hadn't ridden her for ages, but I knew that I had to get up there and be present, and exercise the correct amount of control, and if I did all of that, there was nothing to fear. I didn't need to worry about what the horse was going to do. I didn't have to read

Delilah's mind because I was able to actively do my fifty percent of the relationship.

When I went to pay for my round in the competition, Padraig said, "And you'll want Cathal," and I said, "Can I have Delilah?" and he said, "Either one!" and so I found myself going to get Delilah, who looked surprised to see me. I put on her bridle, reset her saddle, and led her down to the indoor to warm up.

I had forgotten just exactly how stiff this mare was, and it was a bit of a struggle to sit back into the canter. She gave me her leads without a fight though, so that was something. Delilah and I were surrounded by a bunch of little girls, but I didn't feel ashamed about being the only grownup jumping the course set at two feet. I was going at my own pace, and that was that.

Someone put up a cross-rail, and we had a go—Delilah refused the second pass we took. Shit! I was *this close* to putting her back and getting Cathal...but I went at the fence again, and we went over, and it felt okay. A few more jumps, and then I thought, No, that's enough, let's just do this, and off we went to go jump a whole course in front of people.

I had, of course, competed Delilah before in my very-first-ever-show-jumping competition—the one where I missed the fifth fence. Back then I had been working with her regularly. Now it was over a year since I'd ridden her, but as I walked her down to the lower arena where the course was set, I felt good. I felt like I had had plenty of experience with her, and that she had been good to me when I was healing, and that for crying out loud, the fences were really small, so I was—we were—going to be fine.

I wondered, as we walked, about that time, four years before. It had been my first experience of being "a lady on a horse," sitting around and chatting, of being up there—on the horse, in the arena, at the barn for something other than a lesson—and it was like a miracle. Sure, it took me four years to go back and do it again, but it was only because maybe I had finally learned to understand my limits without making them limitations. Giving myself that time in between competitions was a miracle of forgiveness for my *self*.

After all, who blanked out on Fence Number Five? Who's fault was that? Who married a dude who demonstrated, through his actions and well before the nuptials, who he was, quite clearly? I went into that deal with eyes slit open the tiniest bit, and my brain going, *Wow, seriously?* and my heart going, *But, but, but!* I could punish myself for that forever, but I...I stopped. Because there was actually a person there, not just an ex, and he had all his own shit and all his own crazy to deal with; and I knew I did, too.

And sometimes people make poor choices.

Divorce is no joke. I had a flippant attitude toward it until it happened to me, and then it brought with it all sorts of shame and other crap feelings. It was not just about signing a bunch of papers. It was a huge deal, and it was a lot of pain.

I've learned to trust and adhere to a still, small voice inside me. Some may call it a higher power, God, Buddha, Jesus, Mother Mary, Holy Spirit. Getting hung up on the term is a great way to divert your attention from the actual thing itself, from the actual authority to which you have access. I'm not so concerned about putting the "right" name on it—it's enough to realize that one can actually trust this voice, this instinct, this intuition. That realization is, as The Program calls it, a spiritual awakening.

One day when I was at the barn, it was properly summertime hot, for a change, and the horses were feeling it. I went to say hello to everyone and saw that Dancer was lying flat out on his side in his stall. He was smacking his lip, and I felt a rush of nostalgia—my ex had done the same sort of thing, jokingly, when he was pretending to fall asleep. I felt that thought, and I think I may have made an audible sound in reaction to it, because Dancer surged to his feet and came over to stand in front of me, his head over the door.

Dancer had *never* come over and hung his head over the door with me before, at least not in order to receive pets and strokes. He would come over in an intimidating way, sure, maybe to see if you had anything to put in his mouth, and failing to find a carrot or an apple, he might make a grab for your hair, or your fingers, fingers that were trying to scratch and love on him like he was a normal horse, for God's sake.

But that day, he just stood there, his head right near mine, and I put my hand on his face, between his eyes, underneath his surfer-dude forelock. I had never touched his face before, ever. I apologized then, aloud, for having in any way, shape, or form projected any of my shit with my ex-husband onto him, that day, or any day. I apologized from my heart, and said that I would never, ever do it again.

Dancer stepped back into his stall and shook himself from nose to tail, vigorously and completely. He snorted, and I said thank you, and we stood there looking at each other for a while. I felt as humble as I ever have, in all my life.

They may be my spiritual awakening, but horses are not my higher power. I don't want to project divinity on any person, horse, or thing. I will say this, though: if the gift of horseback riding and The Program is The Now, and if my higher power can only exist and can only be found in The Now, and my only experience thus far in my life of that Now has been through horseback riding, then I think that, at least for the time being, my experience of God is grounded in action. And I'm not talking about busyness or doingness, of avoiding stillness, or anything like that. I am talking about *right action*, about what is correct for me. For me, it is giving hours of my life over to my connection to horses and to my physical involvement in equestrian sport. Through my breath and my sweat, getting up from my falls and going over my fences, I've found congruence and clarity.

Just as I wanted to meet my equine soulmate like the ladies always described in the books I read, I wanted my spiritual awakening to be the sun breaking through the clouds with a swelling orchestration. I expected an angelic chorus, and I got a gentle sense of peace instead, from the sound of a hoof scraping the concrete aisle of the barn, the sensation of a horse blowing his breath into my nose, the joy of seeing a horse's head pop up over his stall door, ears forward, when I called his name. I realized that knowing what worked for me was enough...and that was pretty much a spiritual awakening, too.

As they say in The Rooms, take what you like and leave the rest.

It did finally hit me, somewhere between the barn and the rest of my life: *I* was the miracle I had waited for, hoped for, known would save me. Nothing, absolutely nothing outside of me would do it. Nope, not even the horses. Because it was not just about me sitting on a horse that made the miracle of me in middle age, it was about me getting myself up there in the first place. It was about me showing up, frigid mornings and roasting hot afternoons. Falling off and getting back on again. It was commitment, and belief, and trust, and allowing myself to feel joy. To believe that joy could continue. It was the realization that I made my own life, every single day, through my responses and decisions and attitudes.

Every single day. I made it. Nobody else. I couldn't wait for magic because the magic was in my choices and my actions.

When I'm on a horse, it's only for an hour at a time. But that is sixty minutes of nothing but me and the horse, and the lesson, and each individual present moment.

Sometimes, it may look like the moments are all the same. I mean, there you are, trying to ride a good twenty-meter circle, and you're not going to stop just because you didn't get it right the first time. What's best is to be sure that your intention is to progress and not to be perfect. You need to be able to let go of the last twenty-meter circle and move on to the next one. If you are worrying about the last one, you may not even realize that you are in the midst of the best one you've ever ridden, and it would be a shame to miss out on that.

I was going to do the best I could, and I was not going to miss that fifth fence this time round. We walked the course, and Delilah was grooving, her head down and bobbing. There was Fence Number Five, green and white poles. There it is, I said to myself. "Hey," I said aloud to Delilah. "That's Number Five." She flicked an ear at me and snorted.

I watched a few of the little girls jump their rounds, just to get the rhythm of the course, to see what it looked like, what it might feel like. While we waited, Delilah pinned her ears back at every opportunity, and at one stage started dancing backward. Someone from the ground called out helpful advice, and I walked Delilah around in circles behind the horse trailers lined up along the C end of the arena. It dawned on me that it would be good to get going, to not make her stand and wait any longer, so when Padraig called out, "Who's next?" I replied, "Me!" We passed the exiting rider; Delilah made a nasty face at the horse.

I don't really remember jumping that course, the last Saturday of The League. It was eight fences, and if you went clear, you did the first six over again. So, there was the first fence at F, and then the second and third were at a related distance at X, then it was over to the fourth fence at E, then back around to F for the line into a double combination at X for Fence Number Five, then *eeeeeeeeeeeeeek*, a tight turn at H around to six at M, where the first fence became the seventh, and the fourth fence became the eighth.

I do remember Delilah shaking her bum and trying to take off as we trotted large around the arena, and how I thought, Well, if she's hot, she'll be strong and get us over the fences, and then I decided, No, I want to ride this properly. I sat back, determined not to let her get out of hand. I do remember that I was still worried about that effing fifth fence and that I was thinking, Oh, God, I am bouncing around like a sack of potatoes, so I sat back more fully. We must have jumped the effing fifth fence because the next thing I knew we were coming around the turn at H, heading for the sixth and hearing another of my lesson pals call encouragement. I remember going over six and looking ahead and thinking, Oh, there's seven! and feeling surprised by it.

When I landed after the eighth fence, I heard Padraig call, "Clear round!" and so I just kept going, doing the first six over again. As I came around to fence number four, I felt myself losing my left stirrup, and I put more weight in the right stirrup and wiggled my foot to keep the left. I thought, Holy shit, I think we may make it...

And then suddenly we were sailing over the final fence.

The minute we landed, the cheers erupted—friends, lessonmates, teachers, spectators. I felt like my whole body was my heart, beating and beating and full of pure, unadulterated joy.

It was not simply about having gone double clear (although that was pretty spectacular). It was not about winning or looking good in public. It was not about anything having to do with ego, even though you'd think it was kind of all about that. No, my joy came from the pure action that had occurred in the arena, intrinsic via instincts that I had learned: I had learned to ride. I had learned to pay attention. I had learned to communicate clearly. I had learned to not worry about doing a whole thing at once but to do it one step, one stride, one jump at a time. I had learned to look up, to be aware, to contain what needed containing in a manageable way, and to flow forward without fear. This was the triumph of the present moment, of true connection with another being, and in that connection, gaining access to every single pure, beautiful thing in the world, all the way up to God.

Dare I say it? It was completely holy. We can use the term as it relates to all things higher and more powerful, and we can also use it as it refers to *wholeness*, to having been made complete. Everything came together in that series of moments, and I was completely and totally there, without trying too hard, without trying hard at all. I did a thing I had never ever imagined myself doing in the whole of my life, and if that is not a miracle, then I don't know what is.

I whispered to Amy, "Do you think I get a ribbon?"

When the names were called to come forward for the prize-giving, mine was one of them, and I waded through all the little girls like Gulliver.

I tucked the prize carefully into my pocket, and whenever anyone so much as said the word "ribbon," I'd slip my hand in and make sure it was still there.

There it is, I assured myself. There's mine. I had done it. I had gone clear.

FORWARD

It has not escaped my notice that horseback riding dovetails
not-so-nicely with many of my character defects: trying too hard,
aka perfectionism; throwing myself, sometimes literally, into situations that can cause me harm; commitment no matter the regard
to my best interests; projecting any of the above onto others.

So where does that leave me? Have I gotten anywhere at all?

Each of the things that are potentially bad for me have
something to recommend themselves: With my ego out there
on display, every time I can correct my behavior without falling
down a poor-self-esteem rabbit hole, I improve. Every time I
take responsibility for something I've done—dropped the contact,
failed to sit back, found my jumping position too soon/too late—I
improve. Every time I take my own health and safety into consideration, I improve.

Because of my ongoing outside-the-arena fear, I took a
cross-country lesson at an equestrian center in County Wicklow
dedicated to jumping obstacles in fields. I was given a horse that
I felt, immediately, was well up for it. He shuffled his feet in
anticipation as we waited for the rest of the group to mount, his
ears flicking all over the place. Any time I so much as twitched
my leg, he moved. We warmed up in the arena, and all was going

well until the canter—I couldn't get him to *stop* cantering. All the incorrect things I hadn't done in years, I did: hands went up, seat did not go back, bit was leaned on. I hadn't felt like this since Maverick. My amygdala went *hey, hey, this is familiar!* and started flipping through memories of canters that had swiftly gone out of control; luckily, my hypothalamus and I recalled when I'd had a good outcome.

The instructor looked at me as I turned into the center. "How are you doing?"

"Not great," I said. "I'm having trouble with the downward transition from canter."

"Go again, I'll have a look."

We went again. We got rid of my whip. Tried the opposite direction. It seemed like he got faster every time I tried something different. I turned into the center again.

"Better?" she asked.

"No," I replied.

Off him I got, then onto a skewbald mare with ginormous ears called Pumpkin. We had a bit of a trot, a bit of a canter, a bit of a jump—and in far less time than I had on the antsy gelding, I was off into the field. I knew the mare and I were a better match. I jumped a whole bunch of fences the sort I'd never tried before, and we even negotiated a bank successfully, three times out of three. (A pile of earth with a sheer drop on the other side—I thought I was going to die, until I didn't.)

I improve, and not just at riding or horsemanship. When faced with a choice that is hard for me, one that scares me and triggers my people-pleasing tendencies, and I make it anyway, I improve. When I manage not to offer an unsolicited opinion and eschew the opportunity to be that selfless oracular know-it-all, I improve. When I resist the temptation to gossip or criticize, when I don't overreact and I respond instead, when I move on from a relationship that's not congruent with my values, when I resist the desire to chase an unavailable man, I improve.

Improving, I have found, is not so much changing who I am essentially as it is keeping everything in perspective and using common sense. And yet as I change my behaviors, I reveal more of my unadulterated essence, the assets that had become defects of character from trying to cope: I am disciplined, I am focused, I am respectful. When I am less-than-perfect, I am fully human, and should I occasionally backslide and reach for a codependent coping mechanism, well, that too shall pass.

All this does pass, even the euphoric ribbon-winning moments, and even the bad lines to fences. Once, I was riding Delilah and came around to the first element in a combination, and it was not the best approach, and I was berating myself all the way to the second fence for the bad approach to the first one, and guess what? The second jump wasn't great, either. Roisin asked me what I thought went wrong, and I told her that my line was off, and that I knew my line was off, and she said it was good that I realized that—but now I needed to learn to put that behind me, move on, and not take a problem in one place all the way to the next fence.

On Mufasa, who came to Kilternan as a five-year-old, I realized I had gotten into the bad habit of expecting the horse to figure out things, like the number of strides in between fences, basically assuming he could get us where we needed to go. This did not have a good outcome as far as Mufasa was concerned. He was so young that he needed me to guide him—me! Guide *him*! The more experienced horses I'd ridden in the past (yes, even Maverick) went some way toward covering up my inexperience. But faced with yet another jump combination, I had to ride Mufasa, entirely present, every step, all the way through. It wasn't perfect, and once, I had to solve a problem seemingly in mid-air, but I was proactive, and Roisin said, "You recovered well, where before you would have just sat there."

So there is a difference between sitting back and just sitting there? Okay.

Everything about my recovery and my riding has been about learning, about becoming "teachable," which is such a Program term I cringe a little, but it is in line with the principles of twelve-step, and equally in line with the joys I get out of my sport. I learned about gratitude in The Rooms. I am grateful that I kept going back, with an open mind; that I've learned to ask for help; for my capacity to learn, and for my lifelong desire to do so.

I never did buy myself a horse—or at least I haven't yet. I occasionally go mooching round the web and hit the sales sites, looking at pictures and videos, wondering if I could really love a horse called Bernard (I totally could!) or if that mare who looked good over fences might be the one for me. I still feel like I'm not ready to settle down, so instead of forcing the issue, I'm waiting. I'll know when I know. There is, for once, no rush.

A dressage arena is twenty by forty meters, which is generally smaller than a normal arena would be, with lengths of white plastic laid out in a rectangle and the letters set at their proper points. When performing a dressage test, marks are based on "10" for each movement, with the number of requirements dependent upon the test's level of difficulty; also judged are the horse's paces, submission, and the rider's position, seat, and correct application of aids.

There had been any number of times in which my instructors attempted to incorporate a dressage test into a lesson. Sure, we'd always do loads of flatwork, but it never got its own time to shine, unless we tried to do a test. *Tried* being the operative word because what generally happened was: we'd get the test and take it away to memorize it, come back the next week and practice it with the instructor correcting us as we went along, but maybe one or two riders didn't show up that week, so we'd resolve to do it all over again the next. The one or two who missed might show up this time, but the weather would be dreadful, and no one would want to stand around in the rain, waiting for their turn to ride the test. So it would be put off again.

And then one or two riders wouldn't show up the next week, or all the arenas would be booked for something else so the white boundary markers couldn't be laid out properly...and then the week after *that*, there might be a jumping course still set up from pony camp and we'd all prefer to do that instead...

So the dressage test never got done.

We were given a sheet with the required movements by Eileen, our new instructor: a simple, pre-novice test. As always, it was strange to have to learn what I needed to ride in my mind first—you have to know the transitions in your head before you can do them with your body. It doesn't work to ride with the test in one hand and the horse in the other (I tried). I drew a rectangle on a blank piece of paper, muttering *All King Edward's Horses Carry Many Brave Fools* as I set out the letters from the ring. Then I "sketched" the test in my hand-drawn arena, moving my pen faster for canter, slower for walk, and somewhere in the middle for trot. I spent a lot of time during my commute tracing the test on my palm: enter at A, track left at C, twenty-meter circle at B....There was always a moment where it felt like my brain went on hold after the first canter (When do we transition down to walk?), and the picture in my head would go all fuzzy the way TVs used to when the signal went out. But somehow I'd tune back in again and carry on.

The week after we got it, we practiced the test in our lesson...but then with all the usual myriad delays, after six weeks, we forgot about it. I had the sheet, folded up into eighths, in the pocket of my jodhpurs, and then finally gave up and left it at home. The very next Wednesday, as we all mounted for our evening lesson, Eileen said, "Head on out to the upper arena. We're doing the test."

Seriously? Everyone looked at me, because I always had the test sheet, and I said, "I don't have the sheet!" and we moaned, communally. As we filed up to the arena, we quizzed each other: What happened after the walk from F to H on the loose rein? What were we meant to do after that last canter? Did we just head straight up from A to C for the final halt or did we have to go around and change direction and *then* halt?

The atmosphere was very much the way I imagined a proper competition to be. We didn't warm up all together, we had to cope with nerves, we had to line up along one side of the white plastic boundary, and trot around it (alone) before we entered. I was going second, and I was glad I was getting it over with. It was hot (Cathal's coat was black and therefore, I felt, more susceptible to the heat than the other horses'), the sun was glaring, forcing me to squint—oh, the excuses were mounting!

Honestly, though, I felt confident. Cathal had been surprisingly good when we practiced. His circles were nice and round, even in the canter (and that was quite a feat given his first attempts, and I felt good about how far he'd come, and how I'd helped him get there).

The first rider did her test and then it was our turn. I moved Cathal away from the other horses and asked for the trot. Off we went, around the white boundary, waiting for Eileen to let us know we should enter and begin. But it took longer for her to score the previous rider's test than I'd thought...was Cathal going to tire? I brought him back down to walk, but then thought, Am I confusing him? So I asked for trot again. (If he wasn't confused before, he certainly was now.) Soon enough we were trotting in at A.

All I could hear was my breath and the beat of Cathal's hooves. The space outlined by the white barriers felt super-extra-small, since we'd never ridden within the proper dimensions before. For all I knew, Cathal would spook and dance away from the markers, or maybe walk all over them. This inspired some of the best outside leg I've ever applied.

When we were cantering the first circle at C, I thought to myself, We are totally crushing this! Then, at one stage, he did almost step on one of the white barriers (from the brain to the rein!), and I wasn't crazy about the way we transitioned to the second canter, on the left rein between A and F, but otherwise...I was delighted. By the time we halted and saluted at X, it was with a mixture of assurance and glee.

We got our marks and scores as we dismounted down at the barn; I kept my cool even though I spotted four "10s" on my test sheet. Cathal got the biggest pat of his life, and I was chattering at him the whole time I untacked him and put him to bed. He just wanted his treat, which he received: one well-earned Pink Lady apple (his preference).

The perfectionist in me is always going to respond to a good score (four "10s"!), but the rider in me was purely ecstatic about the progress Cathal and I had made. I was pleased that all the work I'd put into him had come good and that he seemed to have enjoyed the experience, too. It was amazing to feel him doing so well—and I knew that my riding was improving when he did what I asked (because I was finally asking properly). My aids were spot on, and the pressure of the test and the element of competition kept me focused. I resolved to look up other dressage tests online and see what the next level looked like. I was glad I hadn't written off the discipline entirely and looked forward to pursuing it in greater depth.

I said goodnight to Cathal and turned to leave the barn, done for the night, and ready to do it all over again the next time, always ready to learn the next thing. Horseback riding is never done: I end where I began, in a stall that needs shit-shoveling, at the top of yet another twenty-meter circle—I do it all again, somewhat differently, perhaps more correctly, learning from my mistakes and building on my successes, one day at a time.

ABOUT THE AUTHOR

Susan E. Conley has a Master of Philosophy in Irish Theatre Studies from the Samuel Beckett Centre, Trinity College, an Honours Degree in Psychology, and a diploma in Equine Assisted Therapy and Learning. Conley is the author of three other books: *Drama Queen*; *The Fidelity Project*; and *That Magic Mischief*. You can follow Susan on Twitter and Instagram @manybravefools and read her blog about horses and writing at manybravefools.com.

ABOUT THE COVER PHOTOGRAPH

The front cover photograph is by international fashion photographer Donna DeMari. DeMari—the first woman to shoot the *Sports Illustrated* swimsuit issue, and a longtime editorial contributor to *Italian Vogue, Marie Claire, Elle,* and *L'Officiel,* among others—has been photographing horses for more than two decades. Her horse photographs have been gracing the walls and windows of Ralph Lauren stores around the world for the last ten years.

The American-born DeMari bought her first camera at the age of eighteen after signing up for a photojournalism course in college. DeMari spent several years in New York, eventually moving to Europe, where she spent fifteen years living between Paris, London, and Milan, shooting fashion editorial during the golden age of the supermodel. During the years that her lens turned upon such well-known persons as Kate Moss, Heidi Klum, Tyra Banks, Naomi Campbell, Christy Turlington, Linda Evangelista, and others, DeMari photographed equine subjects wherever she encountered them, the result of a love affair with horses that began at the age of four.

After returning permanently to the United States, DeMari has increasingly focused on photographing horses, bringing her fashion aesthetic and intimate style to her equine subjects.

DeMari has shown her work in numerous exhibitions and has published six books of photographs. She has been featured in segments on ABC and VH1 Television, and was the subject of an episode of the *Equestrian Life* series, "For the Love of the Horse." For more information about Donna DeMari, visit www.donnademari.com.

ACKNOWLEDGMENTS

Thanks to the Infant of Prague, who did fix it.

Thanks to my "pony mom" Nancy, and the rest of my family, who support me in all I do, and in loving memory of my father John, and my godmother, Auntie Sue.

I wouldn't be writing about horses today if it wasn't for the excellent standard of instruction I've enjoyed in the last twelve years—and I definitely wouldn't have gotten anywhere at all if Nici O'Brien hadn't let me stay in walk for the entirety of my first lesson. Having let me do what I wanted—or not do, as was the case—she encouraged me to come back for another lesson. Ruth Shanahan, Emma Cahill, Fiona Richardson, Sue Carroll, Paul O'Leary, Bernadette Dunne, and Jackie O'Toole have all had an influential hand in keeping me in the saddle, as have Karen, Lynne, Lisa, and many others: thanks a million, lads.

Enormous thanks to Linda Monaghan for allowing her boy to figure largely in this book.

Helping me to become a horse person are the friends I made along the way: my lessonmates, especially the ones who've made it easier for me to get up and down that long, long road: Anne-Marie Kilcullen, Claire Phelan, Lorraine and Lainey, Sharon Kennedy, Elisabeth Lantz, Marie Rostan, Rachel O'Neill, Marijke Sleven, and the countless others who were generous enough to drop me down to the church off the N11, much less all the way home.

Thanks to my non-horsey pals: Karen Fricker, Taylor Zada, Wendy Elliott, Susan Marro, Siobhan Colgan, Shauna O'Halloran, Brenda McCormick, Heidi Vambeck, and Dee O'Keeffe, all of whom bridge both sides of this story. My deep, heartfelt gratitude for everything.

Much appreciation to Sandra Cooke and Ciara O Dowd for insightful and encouraging beta reads; to Maryjane Fahey for recommending Mark Chimsky, the unflagging support from the former (over many, many years!) and the incisive edit from the latter helped me, and the work, immeasurably; to Michelle Dardis for witnessing the signing of my contract and keeping it on the down low.

Thank you, Trafalgar Square Books, for everything, and I mean everything: from the gracious, immediate response to my query, for the time taken to consider it, for choosing to work with me, and for the warm and professional process bringing *Many Brave Fools* to bear has been. Thanks, Martha Cook, for your patience in going over the contract; Rebecca Didier for a beautiful cover and a superb edit that focused and sharpened the message; Caroline Robbins, Publisher; designer Tim Holtz; and all who make TSB a leader in equine literature. I am humbled and grateful to number among your authors.

And finally, the horses. We feed them and shelter them in return for the privilege to ride them. They are often mistreated and taken for granted. Whatever we've done to deserve them, I'm not entirely sure, but not a day goes by that I don't marvel at the difference they've made in my life, and wish that everyone could experience that, too.

NOTES

1 Beattie, Melody. *Codependent No More: How to Stop Controlling Other and Start Caring for Yourself.* Center City, MN: Hazelden Foundation, 1987.

2 *ibid.*

3 Dorrance, Bill with Desmond, Leslie. *True Horsemanship Through Feel.* Washington, DC: Lyons Press, 2nd Revised edition, 2007.

4 Katsamanis, Dr. Maria. "Marwari of USA: Jewels of Antiquity." Going Gaited Online Magazine, August 2010, www.goinggaited.com.

5 Smiley, Jane. *A Year at the Races: Reflections on Horses, Humans, Love, Money, and Luck.* London, England: Faber and Faber Limited, 2004.

BIBLIOGRAPHY

Ackerman, Sherry. *Dressage in the Fourth Dimension*. Novato, California: New World Library, 2008.

Al-Anon Family Groups

—One Day at a Time in Al-Anon. Tunbridge Wells, Kent: KSC Printers, 1992 (1968).

—Hope for Today. Canada, 2002.

Allen, Linda L., with Dennis, Dianna R. *101 Jumping Exercises for Horse & Rider*. Cincinnati, Ohio: David & Charles Ltd, 2004, 2006.

Anderson, Allen and Linda. *Angel Horses: Divine Messengers of Hope*. Novato, California: New World Library, 2006.

Bagnold, Enid. *National Velvet*. London, England: Egmont UK Ltd, 2007. (1935)

Beattie, Melody

—*Beyond Codependency: And Getting Better All the Time*. Center City, MN: Hazelden Foundation, 1989.

—*Codependent's Guide to the Twelve Steps*. New York, NY: Fireside (Simon & Schuster), 1990.

—*Codependent No More: How to Stop Controlling Others and Start Caring for Yourself*. Center City, MN: Hazelden Foundation, 1987.

—*52 Weeks of Conscious Contact: Meditations for Connecting with God, Self & Others*. Center City, MN: Hazelden Foundation, 2003.

Coates, Margrit. *Horses Talking: How to Share Healing Messages with the Horses in Your Life*. London, England: Ebury Press, 2005.

Codependents Anonymous, *CoDA*. Dallas, TX: CoDA Resource Publishing, 1995.

Conley, Kevin. *Stud: Adventures in Breeding*. London, England: Bloomsbury, 2002.

Constantino, Maria, and Lang, Amanda. *Complete Horse: A Highly Informative Guide to the World of Horses*. Wigston, Leicester, UK: Silverdale Books, 2006.

Csikszentmihalyi, Mihaly, *Flow: The Psychology of Optimal Experience*. New York, NY: HarperPerennial, 1990.

Dreisbach, Verna, Ed. *Why We Ride: Women Writers on the Horses in Their Lives.* Berkeley, California: Perseus Books, 2010.

Dorrance, Bill with Desmond, Leslie. *True Horsemanship Through Feel.* Washington, DC: Lyons Press, 2nd Revised edition, 2007.

Edwards, Elwyn Hartley. *Horses.* London, England: Dorling Kindersley Limited, 1993.

Gloss, Molly. *The Heart of Horses.* London, England: Pan Macmillan Ltd, 2009.

Golding, Wendy. "The Science of It All." www.equineleadership.ca, 2018.

Goudge, Elizabeth. *The Little White Horse.* Oxford, England: Lion Hudson plc, 2008. (1946)

Henderson, Carol. *Teach Yourself: Owning a Horse.* London, England: Hodder Education, 2006.

Hill, Cherry. *How to Think Like a Horse.* North Adams, Massachusetts: Storey Publishing, 2006.

Hillenbrand, Laura. *Seabiscuit.* London, England: Harper Collins Publishers, 2001.

Irwin, Chris. *Horses Don't Lie: What Horses Teach Us About Our Natural Capacity for Awareness, Confidence, Courage, and Trust.* New York, New York: Avalon Publishing Group Incorporated, 1998, 2002.

— with Weber, Bob. *Dancing with Your Dark Horse: How Horse Sense Helps Us Find Balance, Strength and Wisdom.* New York, New York: Avalon Publishing Group Incorporated, 2005.

Isaacson, Rupert. *The Horse Boy: A Father's Miraculous Journey to Heal His Son.* London, England: The Penguin Group, 2009.

Kohanov, Linda. *The Tao of Equus: A Woman's Journey of Healing & Transformation through the Way of the Horse.* Novato, California: New World Library, 2001.

—*Riding Between the Worlds.* Novato, California: New World Library, 2003.

Korda, Michael. *Horse People: Scenes form the Riding Life.* New York, New York: HarperCollins Publishers, 2003.

Marks, Kelly. *Perfect Manners: How You Should Behave So Your Horse Does Too.* London, England: Ebury Press, 2002.

McBane, Susan. *100 Ways to Improve Your Riding: Common Faults and How to Cure Them.* Cincinnati, Ohio: David & Charles Ltd, 2004, 2006.

Mews, Anna Clemence, and Dicker, Julie. *What Horses Say: How to Hear, Help and Heal Them.* Shrewsbury, England: Kenilworth Press, 2004.

Midkiff, Mary D. *She Flies Without Wings: How Horses Touch a Woman's Soul.* New York, New York: Dell Publishing, 2001.

Miller, Joy. *Addictive Relationships: Reclaiming Your Boundaries.* Deerfield Beach, FL: Health Communications, Inc., 1989.

Moffett, Heather. *Enlightened Equitation: Riding in True Harmony with Your Horse.* Great Britain: David & Charles, 1999, 2002.

Myss, Caroline, PhD. *Anatomy of the Spirit: The Seven Stages of Power and Healing.* London, England: Transworld Publishers, 1997.

Pony Boy, Gawani. *Horse, Follow Closely: Native American Horsemanship.* Irvine, California: Bow Tie Press, 1998.

Pipe, Jeff. "Stonewalling in Marital Relationships." www.liveabout.com, 2014.

Price, Steven D., Ed. *The Greatest Horse Stories Ever Told: Thirty Unforgettable Horse Tales.* Guilford, Connecticut: The Lyons Press, 2001, 2004.

Rashid, Mark. *Life Lessons from a Ranch Horse.* Great Britain: Antony Rowe Ltd, 2003, 2004.

Roberts, Monty. *Ask Monty: The 150 Most Common Horse Problems Solved.* London, England: Headline Publishing, 2007.

— *The Horses in My Life.* London, England: Headline Publishing, 2006.

Roth, Gabrielle. Sweat Your Prayers. New York, NY: Newleaf, Gill & Macmillan Ltd, 1997.

Seltzer, Leon F, Phd. "Codependent or Simply Dependent: What's the Big Difference?" www.psychologytoday.com, 2014.

Sewell, Anna. *Black Beauty.* London, England: Puffin Books, 1877, 1954, 1994.

Smiley, Jane. *A Year at the Races: Reflections on Horses, Humans, Love, Money, and Luck.* London, England: Faber and Faber Limited, 2004.

—*Horse Heaven.* London, England: Faber and Faber Limited, 2000.

Strozzi, Arianna. *Horse Sense for the Leader Within: Are You Leading Your Life, Or Is It Leading You?* Bloomington, Indiana: Authorhouse, 2004.

Tellington-Jones, Linda, with Taylor, Sybil. *Getting in TTouch: Understand and Influence Your Horse's Personality.* North Pomfret, Vermont: Trafalgar Square Books, 1995.

Twelveponies, Mary. *There Are No Problem Horses, Only Problem Riders.* New York, New York: Houghton Mifflin Company, 1982.

Walls, Jeannette. *Half Broke Horses.* London, England: Simon & Schuster UK Ltd, 2009.

Widdicombe, Sarah. *Horse Bits & Pieces: Sublime Equine Trivia.* Cincinnati, Ohio: David & Charles Ltd, 2004, 2006.